Lift Every Voice and Sing II

An African American Hymnal

Lift Every Voice and Sing II

An African American Hymnal

CHURCH PUBLISHING INCORPORATED, NEW YORK

Canon 24, Section 1

It shall be the duty of every Minister to see that music is used as an offering for the glory of God and as a help to the people in their worship in accordance with The Book of Common Prayer and as authorized by the rubrics or by the General Convention of this Church. To this end the Minister shall have final authority in the administration of matters pertaining to music. In fulfilling this responsibility the Minister shall seek assistance from persons skilled in music. Together they shall see that music is appropriate to the context in which it is used.

20 19 18 17 16 15 14 13 12 11

This hymnal
is dedicated to the
memory of

The Reverend

Curtis Winfield Sisco, Jr.

1958 – 1992

creative liturgist
gifted musician
devoted priest

Contents

Service Music

Indices

Hymns and Songs

Service Music

Preface

At the outset, the Editorial Committee decided that *Lift Every Voice and Sing II* would contain music drawn from the following genres:

Negro spirituals
Traditional and contemporary Gospel songs
Adapted Protestant hymns
Missionary and evangelistic hymns
Service music and mass settings in both
traditional and Gospel settings

It was later decided to include a section containing hymns for African American saints on the Church's calendar.

The contents of the hymnal were drawn from several sources. The committee chose hymns to be retained from *LEVAS I* and hymns from other black hymnals. Notably, *"Lead Me, Guide Me"* (Roman Catholic) and *"Songs of Zion"* (United Methodist) were consulted as were Caribbean hymnals. Also, since *LEVAS II* is seen to be a supplement to *The Hymnal 1982*, it was decided that with the exception of the "title hymn" and one or two others with unique arrangements, we would not include hymns which are contained in 1982. In addition, it was decided to include several new works (both texts and music) which were subsequently solicited or commissioned.

While the reasons for choosing spirituals and Gospel songs may be obvious, the *raison d'être* for the inclusion of missionary and evangelistic hymns and "adapted Protestant hymns" might need some explanation. Bishop Burgess, in his Preface to *LEVAS I*, observed:

Just as the slaves not only adopted the religion of their masters, but transformed it into a Gospel that had particular meaning for themselves, so the Black Christians have taken the hymnody of the evangelical church and claimed it for their own. These hymns do not have the theological purity of the spirituals, nor do they arise out of the bitter experience of Black people. In adopting this music, again like the Christian religion itself, the Black congregation has used the notation merely as a guide. The free expression of enthusiastic faith has raised this music into a genre that rightly takes its place within Black congregational worship.

The Committee was especially interested in providing mass settings and service music reflective of the black musical idiom. In a survey conducted by the committee at the beginning of the project, such a need was duly noted, since the paucity of such music was seen as a deficiency of *LEVAS I.* The survey also reminded us that almost all black parishes are Eucharistically-centered. Therefore, the decision was made that service music in *LEVAS II* would include only that used in the Holy Eucharist.

The arrangement of the contents of *LEVAS II* is worthy of comment. We were concerned that we keep in mind that in this church we follow a liturgical year and that hymns be used appropriately. There is a fine art in choosing hymns which are theologically and thematically compatible with the liturgy. Hymns which were not composed originally to fit into a liturgical context were studied to determine where they could best be employed. One result of this is that certain hymns have been rescued from obscurity, and others have been given new significance. This arrangement will help planners of worship use hymns germane to a particular season or occasion.

There are so many individuals to whom we owe thanks. We acknowledge first those who have gone before and succeeded in providing for the Episcopal Church the first collection of African American sacred songs—*Lift Every Voice and Sing I.* Particular thanks is expressed to the Rt. Rev. Franklin D. Turner, now suffragan bishop of Pennsylvania. To him, to the Rt. Rev. John M. Burgess, retired bishop of Massachusetts and to Dr. Irene V. Jackson-Brown is expressed appreciation for their determination to complete the first edition of this hymnal. We stand on their shoulders in continuing the work they began.

Lift Every Voice and Sing II is a new musical resource and would not have been accomplished were it not for the tireless efforts of its gifted Editorial Committee. Therefore to them go primary credit and praise for their hours of work too numerous to count.

We are especially grateful to Dr. Horace Clarence Boyer, Professor of Music at the University of Massachusetts, at Amherst, who served creatively and with distinction as General Editor. Dr. Carl Haywood, Professor of Music at Norfolk State University and organist/choir director at Grace Episcopal Church in Norfolk, Virginia served as editor of the service music section and made incomparable contributions toward the completion of this hymnal. Until his death, the Rev. Curtis W. Sisco, Rector of St. Luke's Church in New Orleans served proficiently as liturgical editor and was of immeasurable value on the Committee.

Every Committee member contributed his or her unique gifts. Therefore profound gratitude is also expressed to Dr. Deborah Harmon Hines, the Rev. Dr. Richard C. Martin, Mr. Robert L. Simpson, Mrs. Doris P. Summey (secretary), and Mrs. Irma Tillery.

The Editorial Committee was ably staffed by the Rev. Canon Harold T. Lewis, of the Office for Black Ministries, by Mr. Frank Hemlin, Publisher of the Church Hymnal Corporation and by Dr. Irene V. Jackson-Brown in her capacity as Coordinator of Program Resources at the Episcopal Church Center.

A word of thanks goes to the members of the Union of Black Episcopalians who through their completion of questionnaires, letters and correspondence assisted the Editorial Committee in selecting materials for this collection.

We thank Mr. Marc S. Jones of the Office for Black Ministries who coordinated the copyright process and Mrs. Margaret West of the Church Hymnal Corporation who oversaw the engraving process. Thanks are due to the Rev. Dr. Kortright Davis and to the Rev. Dr. Lloyd A. Lewis, Jr. who reviewed the words of each hymn for theological clarity and to Dr. Carl G. Harris and Dr. Adolphus Hailstork who reviewed the musical texts. The cover design is the result of the artistry of the gifted Dr. Dwight Johnson.

We are grateful to the Episcopal Commission for Black Ministries, the Standing Commission on Church Music and the Church Hymnal Corporation whose cooperation and support brought this effort to completion.

Finally we are indebted to every composer, arranger and lyricist whose work is represented in this collection of African American sacred songs.

We have completed our work trusting that all we have done is to the glory of God. We join in the words of the Psalmist, "*Sing to the Lord a new song; sing his praise in the congregation of the faithful. Let everything that has breath praise the Lord*".

The Rt. Rev. Arthur B. Williams, Jr., D.D.
Chair of the Editorial Board
Bishop Suffragan of Ohio

Introduction

Why an African American Hymnal?

The ways in which a people expresses itself musically and liturgically provide us, perhaps, with the most significant insights into its culture. Believing this, and in an attempt to share some of the gifts that black people bring to the whole church, the Episcopal Commission for Black Ministries, under the aegis of the Church Hymnal Corporation, published *Lift Every Voice and Sing: A Collection of Afro-American Spirituals and Other Songs (LEVAS I)* in 1981. Today, a little more than a decade later, in collaboration with the Standing Commission on Church Music, and again under the aegis of the Church Hymnal Corporation, the Episcopal Commission for Black Ministries now offers *Lift Every Voice and Sing II: An African American Hymnal (LEVAS II).*

While it is not within the scope of this introduction to give a comprehensive overview of church music among black Episcopalians, a few observations might enable us to better understand the place of *LEVAS II* in that historical evolution. There is an old French proverb: "*Plus ça change, plus la même chose.*" ("The more things change, the more they remain the same.") This adage seems applicable to the development of church music among black Episcopalians. In an article entitled "Music Among Blacks in the Episcopal Church: Some Preliminary Considerations" which appeared in the *Historical Magazine of the Episcopal Church,* Dr. Irene Jackson-Brown, general editor of *LEVAS I,* writes that in the late eighteenth century, "blacks were . . . beginning to experience musical syncretism within the colonial Church of England. That is, blacks were fusing certain African and African American musical practices with Anglo-American musical practices." She also notes that these "musical practices included the singing of religious folk songs," later to be called spirituals.

The Reverend Professor Robert Bennett of the Episcopal Divinity School, in an article entitled "Black Episcopalians: A History from the Colonial Period to the Present Day," also in the *Historical Magazine,* suggests that at least one spiritual actually originated among black Episcopalians:

> In the south, where the majority of black Episcopalians were to be found and where prior to the Civil War the Bishop of South Carolina claimed more black communicants than white and where black churchmen worshipped in separate galleries or chapels, it was this body which described their plantation Holy Communion services in the spiritual, 'Let us break bread together on our knees.'

After the introduction of the organ, many black congregations enjoyed reputations for excellence in church music. From the choir stalls of such places as St. Thomas', Philadelphia (founded by Absalom Jones); St. Philip's, New York City; St. James', Baltimore; and Calvary Church, Charleston, emanated the sacred strains of psalter and hymnal. It was not uncommon for such congregations, in addition to liturgical music, to offer afternoon and evening concerts featuring anthems and other choral works of great composers. But the works chosen were almost always European in origin. A Swedish visitor who attended a service in a black congregation in 1850, included the following comments in a letter home (and I would add parenthetically that the same observations could have been made in 1950):

> I had in the forenoon visited a negro . . . church belonging to the Episcopal creed. There were but few present, and they were of the negro aristocracy of the city. The mode of conducting the divine service was quiet, very proper, and a little tedious. The hymns were beautifully and exquisitely sung.

We must keep in mind that prior to the Civil Rights Movement of the last generation, "black" was often considered not beautiful at all. Celebrating black heritage was not always understood as the way to success in a society in which the dominant culture established the standards to be equalled or excelled. If this was true in society in general, it was no less operative in the church, and in the Episcopal Church in particular. Thus, Bishop Turner, in his Introduction to *LEVAS I,* could write:

> Unfortunately, Afro-Americans, particularly those in predominantly white churches, have not felt comfortable using their own music in formal church services, but instead relegated this music to use at civil and social gatherings. Although Black Episcopalians could not or would not use spirituals in their formal worship, they constantly hummed and sang these songs in private.

The Civil Rights Movement, it can be argued, gave black Episcopalians the license to reclaim the outward and visible signs of their black heritage; and once again, like their forbears of the colonial era, they began to syncretise the clipped cadences of English church music and the syncopations, improvisations and coloratura of the black musical medium. The Venerable Hartshorn Murphy, Archdeacon of Los Angeles, in his keynote address entitled "Expanding our Horizons through Evangelism", delivered at the national conference of the Union of Black Episcopalians in 1989, put it this way:

> As a result of the civil rights and black consciousness movements, something remarkable happened . . . We as a people, re-discovered the validity of "emotionalism" as a religious expression. Where previously, [black] church ladies in the Episcopal Church would go home on Sunday, remove their veils and gloves and sing and listen to spirituals and gospel music, today, they want to do that in church, at least occasionally.

To be sure, this conversion experience was not a universal phenomenon among black Episcopalians. Black Episcopal congregations, like the church at large, number among their members several converts, who often associated the hymns contained in *LEVAS* with music in their former denominational affiliations. But more and more, spirituals, gospel music and mass settings reflective of the black religious experience are enjoying increased prominence, even in those parishes which in a former age, would have limited its mass settings to Willan and Oldroyd, and whose concerts would have featured Vivaldi's "Gloria" or Stainer's "Crucifixion." More correctly, what is happening now is that these parishes are discovering that they can have their liturgical cake and eat it; they can skillfully blend these various elements into a tasteful and artistic whole; like blacks in the colonial era, they have learned to "syncretise." *"Plus ça change, plus la même chose."*

But clearly, *LEVAS II* is not being published solely to enable previously stuffy black Episcopalians to become "sanctified" ones. It is intended to be a resource for the whole church. For as Archdeacon Murphy observes:

> White people, too, want to rejoice and sing "Blessed Assurance" with abandon. This is especially true of young white children who can't get with the program on Sunday mornings after rocking out to Michael Jackson or Whitney Houston all week.

Faithful to the Episcopal Church's new appreciation of multiculturalism, *The Hymnal 1982,* for which *LEVAS II* will serve as a supplement, is a far more inclusive and representative resource than its predecessor. African, Caribbean, Native American, Hispanic, African-American and other sources have been used, to remind worshippers of the rich diversity of all the people of God. We are pleased that the church's official hymnal includes music, both old and new, reflective of the African American experience, and it is in the spirit of providing additional resources from the black musical experience that *LEVAS II* is offered to the Episcopal church at large as well as to our brothers and sisters in the broader ecumenical community. In so doing, we echo the wish of Bishop Burgess, in the Preface to *LEVAS I:*

> It is the hope of the editors and the Commission for Black Ministries that there will be acceptance far beyond those parishes composed largely of Black people. This music will serve the whole church well, if, in making it its own, it will come to understand something more of the mission of all people in today's world.

The history and theology of the black church are embodied in its music. The music of the black church, then, is the expression of the struggle, the pilgrimage and the joy of a people. In an age in which all members of the church are searching for a renewed sense of spirituality, it seems altogether fitting and proper to look to the music of a people whose religious folk songs are for good reason called spirituals. I commend to you the riches of the black musical experience, and express the hope that together we may LIFT EVERY VOICE AND SING!

The Reverend Canon Harold T. Lewis, D.D.
Staff Officer for Black Ministries

Hymns and Songs: Performance Notes

The African American religious singing tradition is derived principally from musical practices in Africa, the United States and the Caribbean, and therefore incorporates many and diverse songs and styles. The revised *Lift Every Voice and Sing* reflects this musical diversity through the inclusion of several types of songs. While many of these songs, such as standard Protestant hymns, African and Caribbean songs, "Lift Every Voice and Sing" and "Prayer for Africa" are usually performed as written, others, such as gospel songs and Negro spirituals, are performed in the traditional African American improvised singing style, and therefore warrant some notes on performance practices.

Since the formation of the Fisk Jubilee Singers in 1871, there have been two styles of singing Negro spirituals. The older style is taken directly from the singing of the slaves, and celebrates the nuances of African American folk music, while the newer style is based on European art music practices. Either style is acceptable, but the styles should not be mixed.

To ensure the most meaningful worship experiences with the music of *Lift Every Voice and Sing,* a discussion of pertinent performance practices is herewith provided for consideration.

Voice

A full, free, and sonorous tone is the hallmark of African American singing; therefore, the singer is encouraged to sing with a fully opened throat. A timid or muted sacred singing style does not necessarily connote piety in the traditional African American service. To be sure, there is a cherished tolerance in the African American community for unusual voices, and a *good* singer, one who sings with sincerity and conviction, is preferable to the singer who possesses a *beautiful* voice, but who sings without conviction.

Congregational singing is the means by which diverse individuals and groups worship the Savior as one committed union, and can provide expression for the deepest yearnings. Much of the congregational singing is executed in the responsorial ("call-and-response") manner between a soloist and congregation. The soloist is usually an experienced singer and will deliver the "call" with firmness and conviction. The congregation should be just as firm in delivering the "response," as each part is of equal importance.

Text

Negro Spirituals and gospel songs are, in part, characterized by very few words in the text, and therefore depend upon repetition to convey their message. Originally necessitated by the inability to read and the casual circumstances under which they were created, spirituals contained only a few words so that they could be learned and performed easily. It is not unusual for a spiritual to have only two different lines of text:

> Oh, bye and bye, bye and bye
> I'm gonna lay down my heavy load.

In addition to the text contained in the printed score, additional words and phrases are often interjected during performance. There is, in African American sacred music, a catalogue of *wandering* couplets and quatrains which are employed when extending the performance of a song or when variety of text is desired. In many cases the selected couplet or quatrain will further the message of the song, though this is not necessarily a qualification for selection. The *spirit* and performance will determine the added texts. Among popular couplets and quatrains are:

> My Lord's done just what He said,
> He healed the sick and raised the dead.

If you cannot sing like angels,
If you cannot preach like Paul,
You can tell the love of Jesus
And say He died for all.

The tradition is so strong that the text in the printed score will often be discarded in favor of a popular couplet or quatrain. This practice has found its way into gospel music, and often only the refrain of the original composition is retained. Standard textual interpolations such as "Oh, Lord," "Yes, Lord," and "Hallelujah" may often precede a line of printed text, but will not interfere with the rhythmic pulse of the song.

Dialect has been retained in many of the spirituals included in the hymnal, which necessitates a word of caution. Dialect should never be emphasized nor delivered with more force than other words in the text. "De" (the) is pronounced as written before words beginning with vowels, while it is pronounced as "duh" when used before words beginning with consonants. Sometimes words are shortened to accommodate rhythmic pulses, and at other times extended to lengthen the value of a note. In no case should the singer attempt to correct the language.

While most Negro Spirituals refer to "we" and "us," many gospel songs use "I" and "me." The use of the first person pronoun does not exclude the community, but speaks for the community from the vantage of individual piety.

Melody

Melodies in many Negro Spirituals and gospel songs are set to five tones (pentatonic) or fewer. Others employ the diatonic (seven tone) scale, but with the flatted third, sixth or seventh. These melodies should not be corrected to conform to the diatonic scale, but should be celebrated for their economy and variety. The novice singer may experience some concern when a flatted seventh is accompanied by a diatonic seventh. This soft dissonance is part of the musical fabric of African Americans and can be accommodated with a little practice.

When the spirit of a worship service is especially intense, singers will often embellish (improvise) the melody with additional tones, resulting in an expanded melodic line (see Improvisation below).

Harmony

When accompanied by a chordal instrument, African American folk music employs standard Western European tertian (in thirds) harmony. In *a cappella* singing, however, two additional types of harmony are prominent. The first is *parallel* harmony in which the melody is harmonized by a tone at the interval or a third or sixth, with this intervallic relationship remaining constant throughout the performance of the song. This method of harmonizing does not include contrary and oblique motion, so prominent in western music. The second type of additional harmony is reminiscent of Western European organum of the ninth century, in that intervals of the fourth and fifth are in abundance, while thirds and sixths, the basis of modern music, are rare. Such harmony is usually employed when songs are performed at very slow tempos.

There are very few instances when Negro Spirituals and gospel songs are not sung in harmony, and singers are encouraged to create their own harmony when that printed in the score is not easily singable.

Rhythm

The most distinguishing characteristic of African American music is rhythm, and is no less so in sacred singing. Each beat should be clearly articulated and attacked with authority, accenting the principal pulse in a unit stronger than the others. In other instances the weak beats should be given a stronger accent than the primary and secondary pulses:

1 **2** 3 **4**

This is especially necessary when singing in a moderately fast tempo, as foot patting (see below) usually takes place on strong beats, leaving weak beats without accents.

Placing the accent on weak rather than strong beats is a feature of syncopation, in which the accent is removed from strong to weak beats, or any portion of a beat except the beginning. Syncopation should never be rushed, but executed solidly within the pulse, and with heavy accentuation. Rushing or anticipating syncopation will cause an increase in the tempo. It is therefore necessary to maintain a clear sense of where the pulse lies so that the combination of the two will create the cross rhythm desired.

Experienced singers often employ symmetrical and asymmetrical divisions of the beat as rhythmic counterpoint to the established pulse. The inexperienced singer should maintain the basic rhythm in such situations, as the resultant rhythm will be one of intricacy and complexity, characteristic of African rhythm.

Meter and Tempo

Standard meters, such as 4/4, 2/4 and 3/4 have been employed for most of the songs in the hymnal, and should be performed in the standard manner. Gospel songs, on the other hand, very often employ a meter involving multiples of three. Therefore, regardless of the meter signature assigned, moderately slow and slow gospel songs should be performed in 6/8, 9/8 or 12/8. This means, for example, a song assigned a meter signature of 4/4 should be performed in 12/8 by allotting three pulses to each quarter note. "Come, Ye Disconsolate" is assigned a meter signature of 4/4:

Come,
ye
dis
- con
- so
- late

When performed as a gospel song, it should be executed as:

Come,
ye
dis
- con
- so
- late

Tempo markings have not been indicated in the hymnal, though time and tradition have dictated the tempos at which most of the songs are to be performed. Many of the songs in the hymnal are classified according to tempo, and were assigned tempos when they were created. Negro Spirituals are divided into basically two tempos. The *sorrow* song (e.g. "Steal Away") is performed in a slow, languorous manner, while the *jubilee* song (e.g. "Certainly, Lord") should be performed in a brisk walking tempo. Moderately slow gospel songs (e.g. "Praise Him") should never be performed sluggishly, but in the tempo of a *gospel* waltz, while the shout song (e.g. "I'm So Glad Jesus Lifted Me") should be performed at a fast tempo. Occasionally a congregation will elect the Baptist Lining Hymn style for a song, in which case the song should be performed without a pulse, instead assigning each syllable an amount of time equal to its importance in the text.

While most Negro Spirituals and gospel songs are sung in a tempo long associated with the song, the location of a song within the service may dictate a different tempo. If a jubilee song is used as a response to a prayer, the tempo may be much slower than that employed as an independent song, while a slow song may be given a faster tempo during such an activity as the "Peace." Regardless of the tempo assigned, maintain that tempo, always realizing that beneath the foreground tempo, there is a background tempo to which the singer must pay close attention to insure the lilt and forward motion required.

Improvisation

Altering, rearranging, and spontaneously composing a melodic line to a given harmony are some of the ways in which African Americans personalize music making, both vocally and instrumentally. The process can involve occasionally changing a single tone, substituting different tones for many of the prescribed tones, or completely paraphrasing a melody. In most cases this is not done as a result of knowing other tones of the chord, but by what sounds and feels "right." The experienced singer has a number of stock motives, fragments, or "runs" that can be used in almost any song, and in cases where this is not possible, the singer may simply repeat words or phrases for a number of times. Improvisation is not only applied to the melody, but rhythm, text, and harmony. Adding extra beats during rests, dividing pulses into two accents, or lengthening or shortening a note, adding to or subtracting from words in the original text, and interpolating passing and auxiliary chords to the original harmonies are all features of African American sacred singing.

Along with altering, rearranging, adding, and omitting tones in a given melody, there are timbre variations associated with the African American singing tradition. Among these are the bending of tones, slides, slurs, grunts, wails, runs, turns, chromaticisms, vocables (nonverbal outbursts), screams, and the use of falsetto. Since improvisation is spontaneous, often the singer has no knowledge of what will come forth. Despite this freedom, the singer must always strive to improvise in the style and in the context of the service. Above all, spontaneity is the ruling performance practice in all African American folk singing.

Instruments

While many of the songs in the hymnal might best be accompanied by organ or piano, others may be accompanied by a variety of instruments. There is no prescribed orchestration for gospel songs, but music directors are encouraged to be creative in assigning instruments for such songs. Since most gospel songs are improvised, they are open to accompaniment by any and all instruments. The basic instrument for gospel is the piano. Improvisation in gospel is relatively easy when it is understood that rhythm is much more important than tones. Unless the song is completely unfamiliar to a congregation, the keyboardist need not play the melody, but can provide an improvised accompaniment by dividing quarter notes into eighth notes, employing triplet figures, or play arpeggios. Since there are very few moments of silence in gospel, rests should be filled in with scales or scalar passages, runs, passing tones, turns, upper and lower neighbor tones, single note or octave interpolations, or glissandi. Balance and taste must dictate when and the amount of improvisation that can support a song. In general, if the singers are vocally active, the accompaniment should be subdued. Where there are open spaces in the singing, the keyboardists should fill in those sections. These devices may also be employed on organ. The Hammond organ, with Leslie B-3 speakers, has long been a favorite gospel music instrument. When organ and piano are used simultaneously, a decision regarding the leader and follower should be clearly understood.

The bass guitar is often used to accompany gospel. When a bass is used it should supply the root of the chord, with occasional uses of inversion, and should provide a strong accent on the primary beat of a rhythmic unit. The trap drummer should not only supply a strong primary and secondary beat, but the customary "back beat" as well. Horns may double the melody, but are much more effective playing riffs, countermelodies, descants or obbligatos, always being careful to play during the "response" and not the "call," which is assigned to the leader. Guitars may also double the melody but can be more effective strumming chords. Other percussion instruments, such as cymbals, tambourines, triangles, conga drums, bongos, and maracas are not intended to keep the beat, but are best used to provide variety within the rhythm. Gospel music bases its use of instruments on Psalm 150, where "everything that hath breath," including instruments, should be used to praise the Lord.

Body Rhythm

All African American folk sacred singing is accompanied by a rhythmic movement of the body. Not only does such movement provide greater rhythmic accentuation in the singing, but frees the body from tension and other "weights" that would interfere with worshipping. Handclapping, patting the feet, swaying, nodding the head, raising the arms upward, and shouting ("holy" dancing) are all common activities during traditional worship services. These activities should not be affected but should flow from the body as the singer releases unnecessary inhibitions and becomes more involved in the singing and worship.

African Americans firmly believe that the Lord is pleased when His children come before His presence with a song. For the greatest enjoyment of the songs in this hymnal, singers should follow the proclamation of the prophet: "lift up thy voice like a trumpet."

Horace Clarence Boyer, Ph.D.
General Editor

Service Music: Performance Notes

The service music section offers a diverse sampling of musical settings for use during the Holy Eucharist. Every effort has been made to include settings which embrace the African American musical tradition—spirituals, gospels, blues, jazz. We have also included some music indigenous to Africa, the Caribbean, and the broader Anglican Communion. Though this melange of musical expression offers many possibilities for creative worship, it is our fervent hope that priests, deacons, church musicians, and parish liturgical committees will select music for the eucharist which:

1. affords free expression;
2. promotes congregational participation and a sense of community;
3. captures the essence of the liturgy;
4. enhances spiritual growth and understanding; and
5. develops the parish's musical productivity and potential.

Because the "celebration" involves the entire congregation, the choir, though given some opportunity for individual expression, should maximize its chief function as the congregation's music leader. Therefore, service planners should choose settings that are within the congregation's grasp while occasionally encouraging the choir to introduce new or more difficult settings.

The editorial committee encourages within a single Eucharistic celebration the use of parts of the Mass from a variety of musical styles and genres. Such a practice, we believe, will serve to revitalize the service from Sunday to Sunday.

Following the settings of the *Gloria in Excelsis,* three alternate songs of praise appear which may be substituted freely for the standard *Gloria*. Likewise, additional musical responses follow the *Prayers of the People* and may be used before, during, or after the prayers from the *Book of Common Prayer* or prayers from other sources. In the *Book of Common Prayer,* that which is spoken may also be sung. To this end, we have also included settings for the "Memorial Acclamation," and the "Great Amen."

Psalms

The singing of the Psalms is a tradition born of the early Christian church which, in modern times, has been developed for practical application through Anglican and Simplified Anglican Chants. Of course, their performance in the more solemn and traditional "plainsong" is always an option. Care should be taken not to rush their performance but to govern their singing by the demands of natural flow and the rhythm of the words.

The refrains and Psalms at the end of the service music section are arranged for use at the Holy Eucharist. They may also be used at Morning and Evening Prayer, adding the *Gloria Patri* at the end of the Psalm, if desired (the *Gloria Patri* is omitted at the Eucharist). The Psalm texts and chants are only suggestions, for many of the refrains may be used with other Psalm texts, chants or tones, transposing where necessary. By varying the Psalm texts in this way, certain refrains may be used for several Sundays to foster congregational familiarity.

Simplified Anglican Chants

Simplified Anglican Chants are easily performed and mastered by the average congregation. Though written in four-part harmony, they should be performed in unison by the congregation; however, the choir may sing in parts. Each half verse of the Psalm is sung on the reciting note up to the last accented syllable. The word or syllable in bold print (last accented syllable) should be sung to the corresponding darkened whole note chord in the chant. When the Psalm text contains an odd number of verses, the second half of the chant is repeated for one of the verses.

We commend to you the riches of African American music—past and present—as we worshipfully challenge all to "make a joyful noise unto the Lord."

Carl Haywood, D.M.A.
Service Music Editor

The Editorial Committee

Hymns and Songs

Lift Every Voice and Sing

1. Lift ev - 'ry voice and sing, Till earth and heav - en
2. Sto - ny the road we trod, Bit - ter the chast - 'ning
3. God of our wea - ry years, God of our si - lent

Words: James Weldon Johnson (1871-1938)
Music: J. Rosamond Johnson (1873-1954)

1. ring, Ring with the har - mo - nies of lib - er -
2. rod, Felt in the days when hope un - born had
3. tears, Thou who hast brought us thus far on the
1. ty; Let our re - joic - ing rise High as the list - 'ning
2. died; Yet with a stead - y beat, Have not our wear - y
3. way; Thou who hast by thy might, Led us in - to the
1. skies, Let it re - sound loud as the roll ing sea.
2. feet Come to the place for which our fa - thers sighed?
3. light, Keep us for - ev - er in the path, we pray.

1. Sing a song full of the faith that the dark past has taught us;
2. We have come o - ver a - way that with tears has been wa - tered;
3. Lest our feet stray from the pla- ces, our God, where we met thee;
3
3
1. Sing a song full of the hope that the pres - ent has
2. We have come, tread- ing our path through the blood of the
3. Lest our hearts, drunk with the wine of the world, we for

1. brought us; Fac - ing the ris - ing sun Of our new
2. slaugh - tered; Out from the gloom - y past, Till now we
3. get thee, Shad - owed be - neath Thy hand, May we for -
1. day be - gun, Let us march on till vic - to - ry is won.
2. stand at last Where the white gleam of our bright star is cast.
3. ev - er stand, True to our God, true to our na - tive land.

2

Behold Your God

Oh thou that tell - est good ti - dings to Zi - on, Oh
thou that tell - est good ti - dings to Je - ru - sa - lem:
Lift up your voice with strength, Lift it up don't be a - fraid. Be -
hold your God. A - rise, and shine, for the
light of the world is come. Be - hold your God!

Words: Isaiah 40:9
Music: Kenneth W. Louis

Bye and Bye

3

O bye and bye, bye and bye, I'm gon-na
lay down my heav - y load.
1. Fine
2.
load.
1. I know my robe's gon-na fit me well,
2. O hell is deep and in dark des - pair,
3. O Chris-tian, can't you a - rise and tell,
I'm gon-na
lay down my heav-y load.
1. I tried it on at the
2. So stop, po' sin - ner and
3. That Je - sus hath done
1.gates of hell.
2.don't go there.
3.all things well.
I'm gon-na lay down my heav-y load.
D.C.

Words: Traditional
Music: Negro Spiritual; arr. Edythe Ethelynn Woodruff (b.1970). Used by Permission.

Bet-ter be read - y; Bet-ter be read - y; Bet-ter be
Read - y; read - y

Bet-ter be read - y to try on your
read - y; Read - y to try your
try on your
read - y to try your

1.
2.
Fine
Bet - ter be
1. Oh! rise up chil - dren,
2. What a glo - ri - ous morn - ing
3. O shout you Christ - ians, you'
4. I soon shall reach that
Fine
long white robe! long white robe Hm

Words: Traditional
Music: Negro Spiritual; arr. R. Nathaniel Dett (1882 - 1943)

1. get your crown,
2. that will be,
3. gain - ing ground,
4. gold - en shore,
And by your Sav-ior's
Our friends and Je - sus
We'll shout old Sa-tan's
And sing the songs we
Bet-ter be read- y to try on your
Read-y to try your long white robe! Hm
try on your
to try your
D.S.
1. side sit down.
2. we shall see.
3. king - dom down!
4. sang be - fore.
1.2.3.4. Bet-ter be
Bet - ter be read - y to try on your
Read - y to try your long white robe!
try on your
To try your
Great Day
5
Great day! Great day, the righ-teous march-ing. Great day.

1.
Fine
2.
1. Char - iot rode on the
2. This is the day of
3. We want no cow - ards
4. Going to take my breast-plate,
God's going to build up Zi - on's walls. Zi - on's walls.
1. moun - tain - top,
2. ju - bi - lee,
3. in our band,
4. sword, and shield,
My God spoke and the
The Lord has set His
We call for val - iant
And march out bold - ly
God's going to build up Zi - on's walls!
D.C.
1. char - iot did stop,
2. peo - ple free,
3. heart - ed men,
4. in the field,
God's going to build up Zi - on's walls!

Words: Traditional
Music: Negro Spiritual; harm. J. Jefferson Cleveland (1937-1988)

Christ Is Coming

Christ is com - ing: Pre - pare the way.
Christ is com - ing: Pre - pare the way.
Fine
Fine
D.C.
Christ is coming. Christ is coming.
D.C.

from *Advent Jazz Vespers II*
Music and Word adapt. by Edward V. Bonnemere

I Want to Be Ready

I want _ to be read - y, I want _ to be read - y. ___

Fine
I want _ to be read - y ___ To walk in Je-ru-sa-lem just like John.

1. John said that Je - ru-sa-lem was four-square,
2. When Pe-ter was preach-ing at Pen-te-cost,

Walk in Je-ru-sa-lem just like John.

1. I hope, good Lord, I'll meet you there,
2. O he was filled with the Ho-ly Ghost,

D.C.
Walk in Je-ru-sa-lem just like John. O

Words: Traditional
Music: Negro Spiritual; arr. R. Nathaniel Dett (1882-1943)

Deep ri - ver, my home is o - ver Jor - dan,
Deep riv - er, Lord, I want to cross o - ver in - to
camp ground. Oh don't you want to go to that gos - pel
feast, That prom - ised land where all is peace? Oh
Deep riv - er, Lord, I want to cross o - ver in - to camp ground.

Words: Traditional
Music: Negro Spiritual; arr. Carl Haywood (b. 1949), from *The Haywood Collection of Negro Spirituals,*

9 On Jordan's Stormy Banks

1. On ___ Jor-dan's storm - y banks I stand, _ And cast a wish-ful eye;
2. All ___ o'er those wide - ex - tend - ed plains,_ Shines one e - ter - nal day;
3. No ___ chill - ing winds or poi-s'nous breath _ Can reach that health-ful shore;
4. When shall I reach that hap - py place _ And be for - ev - er blest?

1. To Ca-naan's fair and hap - py land, Where _ my pos - ses - sions lie.
2. There God the Son for - ev - er reigns, And _ scat-ters night a - way.
3. Sick - ness and sor - row, pain and death, Are ___ felt and feared no more.
4. When shall I see my Fa-ther's face, And ___ in God's bos - om rest?

Fine

D.S. Oh, who will come and go with me? I am bound for the prom-ised land.

I am bound for the prom - ised land, _____ I am bound for the prom-ised land;

D.S.

Words: Samuel Stennett (1727-1795)
Music: American Melody; adapt. Rigdon McCoy McIntosh (1836-1899); arr. Norman Johnson

10 Oh! What a Beautiful City

Oh! what a beau - ti - ful cit - y, Oh! what a

beau - ti - ful cit - y, Oh! what a beau - ti - ful cit - y,
1.
Twelve gates - a to the cit - y, Hal - le - lu - jah!
2. Fine
jah! 1. There's three gates in - a the East, three gates in - a the
2. O, my Lord built - a that day, that was just - a fore
1. West; Three gates in - a the North, and three gates in - a the
2. square; wan - ted all - a you sin - ners to meet Him in - a the
D.C.
1. South, mak-ing it twelve gates - a to the cit - y, a - Hal - le - lu - jah.
2. air, 'cause He built twelve gates - a to the cit - y, a - Hal - le - lu - jah.

Words: Traditional
Music: Negro Spiritual; arr. Irma Tillery (b. 1925). Used by Permission.

Prepare Ye the Way of the Lord

Pre-pare ye the way of the Lord.
Pre - pare ye the way of the Lord.

Words: Isaiah 40:3-4, 9
Music: James E. Moore, Jr.

1.- 4.
Final ending
Fine
1. Make straight in the
2. Fill ev - 'ry
3. Go up to a
4. Say to all
1.- 4.
Final ending
Fine
D.S.
1. des - ert a high - way for our God.
2. val - ley, bring all moun - tains low.
3. moun - tain and shout with a loud voice.
4. peo - ple, here is your God.
D.S.

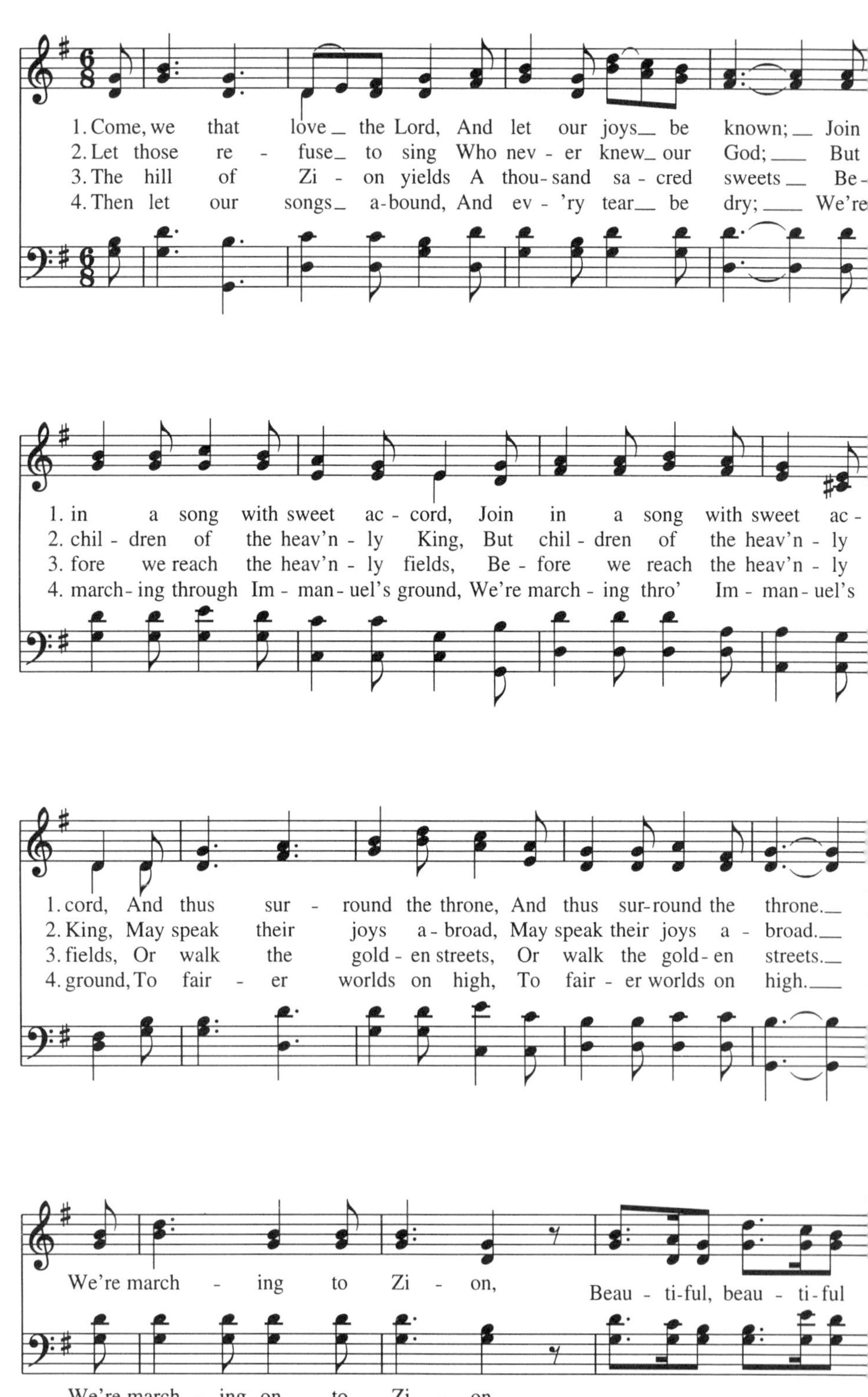
1. Come, we that love the Lord, And let our joys be known; Join
2. Let those re - fuse to sing Who nev - er knew our God; But
3. The hill of Zi - on yields A thou - sand sa - cred sweets Be -
4. Then let our songs a - bound, And ev - 'ry tear be dry; We're
1. in a song with sweet ac - cord, Join in a song with sweet ac -
2. chil - dren of the heav'n - ly King, But chil - dren of the heav'n - ly
3. fore we reach the heav'n - ly fields, Be - fore we reach the heav'n - ly
4. march - ing through Im - man - uel's ground, We're march - ing thro' Im - man - uel's
1. cord, And thus sur - round the throne, And thus sur - round the throne.
2. King, May speak their joys a - broad, May speak their joys a - broad.
3. fields, Or walk the gold - en streets, Or walk the gold - en streets.
4. ground, To fair - er worlds on high, To fair - er worlds on high.
We're march - ing to Zi - on,
Beau - ti - ful, beau - ti - ful
We're march - ing on to Zi - on,

Zi - on; We're march - ing up - ward to Zi - on,
Zi - on, Zi - on,

The beau - ti - ful cit - y of God.

Words: Isaac Watts (1674-1748)
Music: Robert S. Lowry (1826-1899)

My Lord, What a Morning 13

Harmony

My Lord, what a morn - ing, My Lord, what a morn - ing, O

Fine
my Lord, what a morn - ing, When the stars be - gin to fall.

Hymn continues on the next page.

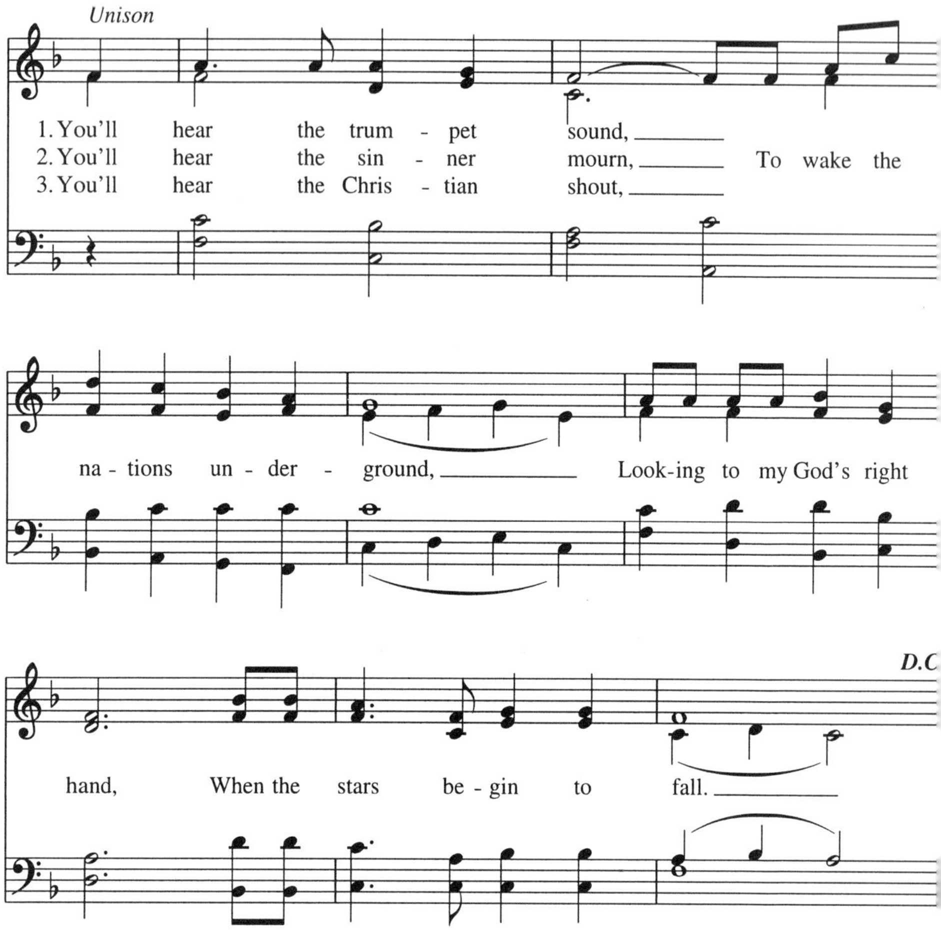

Unison

1. You'll hear the trum - pet sound, ___
2. You'll hear the sin - ner mourn, ___ To wake the
3. You'll hear the Chris - tian shout, ___

na - tions un - der - ground, ___ Look-ing to my God's right

hand, When the stars be - gin to fall. ___

D.C.

Words: Traditional
Music: Negro Spiritual

14 Soon and Very Soon

1. Soon and ver - y soon _ we are goin' to see the King, _
2. No more cry - in' there _ we are goin' to see the King, _
3. No more dy - in' there _ we are goin' to see the King, _
4. Soon and ver - y soon _ we are goin' to see the King; _

Words: Andrae Crouch (b. 1942)
Music: Andrae Crouch

1. Soon and ver - y soon we are goin' to see the King,
2. No more cry - in' there we are goin' to see the King,
3. No more dy - in' there we are goin' to see the King,
4. Soon and ver - y soon we are goin' to see the King,
1. Soon and ver - y soon we are goin' to see the King,
2. No more cry - in' there we are goin' to see the King,
3. No more dy - in' there we are goin' to see the King,
4. Soon and ver - y soon we are goin' to see the King,
Hal-le - lu - jah, Hal - le - lu - jah, we're goin' to see the King!
1. 2.
3. 4.
Hal - le - lu - jah, Hal - le - lu - jah, Hal - le - lu - jah, Hal - le - lu - jah.

15

Climbin' Up d'Mountai

Climb-in'up d' moun - tain, chil - dren.
Good Lawd, Ah
Did-n't come here for to
stay.
Oh, my Lawd, and
If ah nev - er - more see you a-gain, gon-na
meet you at d' judg - ment day
Hal - le - lu - jah, Lawd, Ah'm
1.
2.
Fin
Oh, Lawd,
Oh, Lawd,
1.He - brew chil-dren in de fier - y fur-nace. And dey be-gin to pray, And de
2.Dan - iel went in de li-on's den, And he be-gin to pray, And de
Oh, was-n't dat a might-y
1.good Lawd smote dat fi-yah out.
2.an-gel of de Lawd locked de li-on's jaw.

Words: Traditional
Music: Negro Spiritual; arr. Verolga Nix (b. 1933).

D.S.
day! Good Lawd, was-n't dat a might-y day!
Dat's why Ah'm

You Are Near

16

Yah- weh, I know You are near, stand-ing

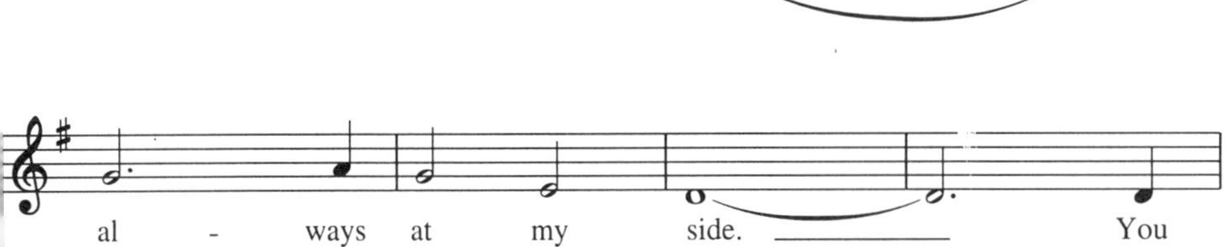
al - ways at my side. You

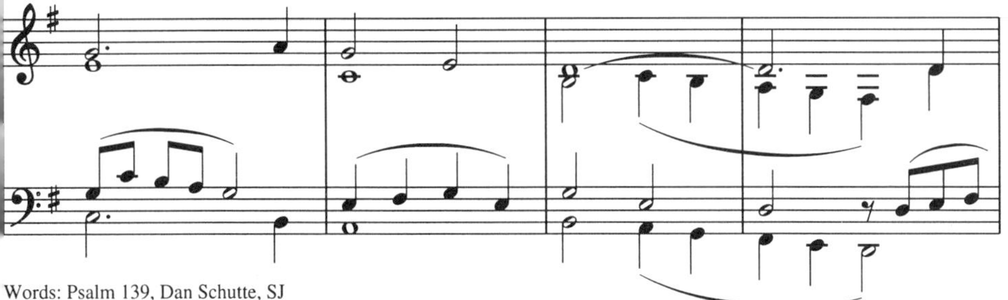

Words: Psalm 139, Dan Schutte, SJ
Music: Dan Schutte, SJ; harm. Theophane Hytrek, OSF

guard me from the foe. And You lead me in

Fine
ways e - ver - last - ing.

1. Lord, You have searched my heart, and You
2. Where can I run from Your love? If I
3. You know my heart and its ways, You who
4. Mar - vel - ous to me are Your works; how pro -

1. know when I sit and when I stand. Your
2. climb to the heav-ens You are there; if I
3. formed me be - fore I was born, in the
4. found are Your thoughts, my Lord. E - ven
1. hand is up - on me pro - tect - ing me from death,
2. fly to the sun - rise or sail be - yond the sea,
3. se - cret of dark - ness be - fore I saw the sun
4. if I could count them, they num - ber as the stars,
D.C.
1. keep - ing me from harm.
2. still I'd find You there.
3. in my moth - er's womb.
4. You would still be there.

Rockin' Jerusalem

O Mar - y, O Mar - tha, O ___ Mar - y, ring dem bells.
O Mar - y, O Mar- tha, O ___ Mar - y, ring dem bells, I
hear arch - an - gels a rock-in' Je - ru - sa- lem, I hear arch-an - gels a
ring - in' dem bells.
Fine
1. Church get-tin' high-er!
2. New Je - ru - sa - lem! __
Rock - in' Je - ru - sa- lem!
1. Church get - tin' high - er!
2. New Je - ru - sa - lem! ____
ring - in' dem bells.

Words: Traditional
Music: Negro Spiritual; arr. Horace Clarence Boyer (b. 1935)

wing Low, Sweet Chariot

Swing low, sweet char - i - ot, Com-ing for to car-ry me home.
Fine
Swing low, sweet char - i - ot, Com-ing for to car-ry me home.
1. I looked o - ver Jor - dan, and what did I see
2. If you get there be - fore I do,
3. The bright - est day that ev - er I saw
4. I'm some - times up and some - times down,
1. Com-ing for to car - ry me home. A band of an - gels
2. Com-ing for to car - ry me home. Tell all my friends I'm
3. Com-ing for to car - ry me home. When Je - sus wash'd my
4. Com-ing for to car - ry me home. But still my soul feels
D.C.
1. com-ing af-ter me, Com-ing for to car - ry me home. O,
2. com - ing too, Com-ing for to car - ry me home. O,
3. sins a - way, Com-ing for to car - ry me home. O,
4. heaven - ly bound, Com-ing for to car - ry me home. O,

ords: Traditional
usic: Negro Spiritual; arr. R. Nathaniel Dett (1882-1943)

1. I'm just a poor way-far - ing stran - ger, I'm trav' - ling through this world be
2. I know dark clouds will gath - er o'er me, I know my path - way's rough and
3. I want to sing sal - va - tions sto - ry, In con - cert with the blood - wash
4. I'll soon be free from ev - ery tri - al, This form will rest be - neath the
1. low; There is no sick - ness, toil, nor dan - ger, In that brigh
2. steep; But gold - en fields lie out be - fore me, Where wea - ry
3. band; I want to wear a crown of glo - ry, When I get
4. sod; I'll drop the cross of self - de - ni - al, And en - ter
1. world to which I go. I'm go - ing there to see my
2. eyes no more shall weep. I'm go - ing there to see my
3. home to that good land. I'm go - ing there to see my
4. in my home with God. I'm go - ing there to see my

Words: Traditional
Music: American Folk Song; arr. Horace Clarence Boyer (b. 1935)

1. fa - ther, I'm go - ing there no more to roam;
2. mo - ther, She said she'd meet me when I come; I'm just a
3. bro - thers, They passed be - fore me one by one;
4. Sav - iour, Who shed for me His pre - cious blood;
go - ing o - ver Jor - dan, I'm just a go - ing o - ver home.

When We All Get to Heaven

1. Sing the won-drous love of Je-sus, Sing His mer-cy and His grace;
2. While we walk the pil-grim path-way, Clouds will o-ver-spread the sky;
3. Let us then be true and faith-ful, Trust-ing, serv-ing ev-'ry day;
4. On-ward to the prize be-fore us! Soon His beau-ty we'll be-hold;
1. In the man-sion bright and bless-ed, He'll pre-pare for us a place.
2. But when trav-'ling days are o-ver, Not a shad-ow, not a sigh.
3. Just one glimpse of Him in glo-ry Will the toils of life re-pay;
4. Soon the pearl-y gates will o-pen; We shall tread the streets of gold.
When we all get to heav-en, What a day of re-
When we all get to heav-en, What a
joic-ing that will be! When we all see
day of re-joic-ing that will be! When we all see
Je-sus, We'll sing and shout the vic-to-ry.
Je-sus, We'll sing and shout, and shout the vic-to-ry.

Words: Eliza Edmunds Hewitt (1851-1920)
Music: Emily Divine Wilson (1865-1942)

Go, Tell It on the Mountain

21

Go, tell it on the moun - tain, o-ver the hills and ev - ery-where;
go, tell it on the moun - tain, that Je - sus Christ is born.
Fine
1. While shep - herds kept their watch - ing o'er si - lent flocks by night,
2. The shep - herds feared and trem - bled, when lo! a - bove the earth,
3. Down in a low - ly man - ger the hum - ble Christ was born,
1. Be - hold through-out the heav - ens there shown a ho - ly light.
2. Rang out the an - gel cho - rus that hailed the Sav - ior's birth.
3. And God sent us sal - va - tion that bless - ed Christ - mas morn.
D.C.

Words: Luke 2:8-20; adapt. John W. Work, Jr. (1871-1925)
Music: Negro Spiritual; adapt. and arr. William Farley Smith (b. 1941)
Words used by permission of Mrs. J. W. Work.

Ma - ry borned a ba - by, Ma - ry borned a ba - by,
Ma - - ry
Ma-ry borned a ba - by, praise His name. _
Mm
What shall we call Him,
Mm
what shall we call Him, what shall we call Him? Praise His name!
Mm
Call Him E-man - uel, call Him E-man - uel, call Him E-man - uel

Words: Traditional
Music: Negro Spiritual; arr. Noah Francis Ryder (1914-1964)

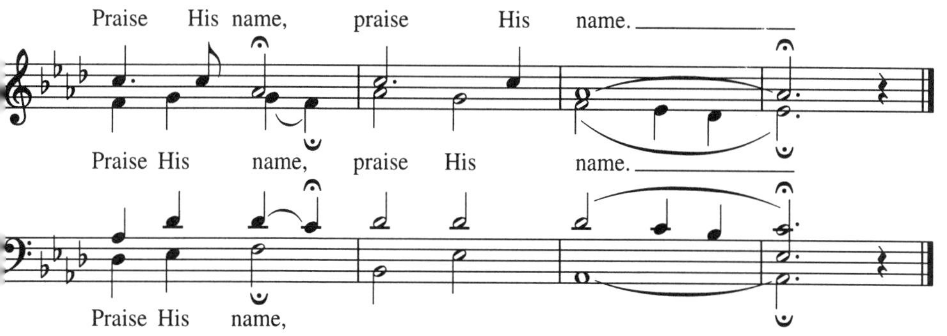
Praise His name, praise His name.
Praise His name, praise His name.
Praise His name,

Jesus Came to Earth from Glory

23

1. Je - sus came _ to earth from glo - ry, That first Christ - mas morn. _
2. As a child, _ the pure and low - ly Gave him great _ de - light. _
3. Grown to man - hood, Pledged to du - ty, Je - sus taught _ and healed. _

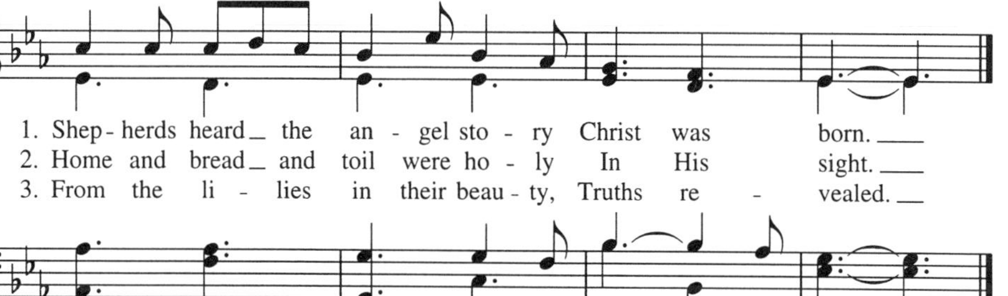
1. Shep - herds heard _ the an - gel sto - ry Christ was born. _
2. Home and bread _ and toil were ho - ly In His sight. _
3. From the li - lies in their beau - ty, Truths re - vealed. _

Words: Hugh Sherlock (b. 1905)
Music: Doreen Potter

Rise Up, Shepherd, and Follow

Unison

1. There's a star in the east on ___ Christ - mas morn,
2. If you take good ___ heed to the an - gel's words,

1. Rise up shep- herd and fol - low, ___ It will lead to the place where the
2. Rise up shep- herd and fol - low, ___ You'll for - get your flocks, you'll for-

1. Christ was born, ___ Rise up shep - herd and fol - low. ___
2. get your herds, ___ Rise up shep - herd and fol - low. ___

Harmony

Fol - low, fol - low, Rise up shep- herd and fol - low, ___

Fol- low the Star of Beth - le - hem, ___ Rise up shep-herd and fol - low. ___

Words: Traditional
Music: Negro Spiritual

'hat Boy-Child of Mary

That boy-child of Ma - ry was born in a sta - ble, a man-ger his
cra - dle in Beth - le - hem.
Fine
1. What shall we call Him,
2. His name is Je - sus,
3. How can He save us,
4. Gift of the Fa - ther,
5. One with the Fa - ther,
6. Glad - ly we praise Him,
D.C.
1. Child of the man - ger? What name is giv - en in Beth-le - hem?
2. God ev-er with us, God giv-en for us in Beth-le - hem?
3. How can He help us, Born here a-mong us in Beth-le - hem?
4. To hu-man moth - er, Makes Him our broth - er in Beth-le - hem?
5. He is our Sav - ior, Heav-en-sent help - er in Beth-le - hem?
6. Love and a-dore Him, Give our-selves to Him in Beth-le - hem?

ords: Luke 2:7; Tom Colvin (b. 1925)
usic: Traditional Malawi Melody; adapt. Tom Colvin (b. 1925)

1. Si - lent night, ho - ly night,
2. Si - lent night, ho - ly night,
3. Si - lent night, ho - ly night,
4. Si - lent night, ho - ly night,
1. All is calm, all is bright Round yon
2. Shep - herds quake at the sight, Glo - ries
3. Son of God, loves pure light Ra - diant
4. All is dark save the light Yon - der
1. vir - gin moth - er and child, Ho - ly in - fant so
2. stream from heav - en a - far, Heav'n - ly host sing
3. beams from thy Ho - ly face, With the dawn of re -
4. where thy sweet vig - gils keep. O'er the Babe who in
1. ten - der and mild; Sleep in heav - en - ly peace,
2. Al - le - lu - ia; Christ the Sav - ior is born,
3. deem - ing grace; Je - sus, Lord, at thy birth,
4. si - lence sleep; Rest in heav - en - ly peace,

Words: Joseph Mohr (1792-1848)
Music: Franz Gruber (1787-1863); arr. Horace Clarence Boyer (b. 1935)

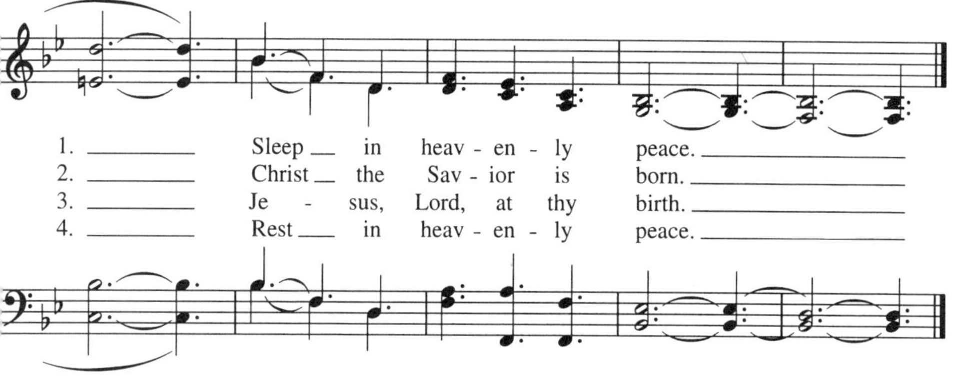
1. Sleep in heav - en - ly peace.
2. Christ the Sav - ior is born.
3. Je - sus, Lord, at thy birth.
4. Rest in heav - en - ly peace.

Away in a Manger 27

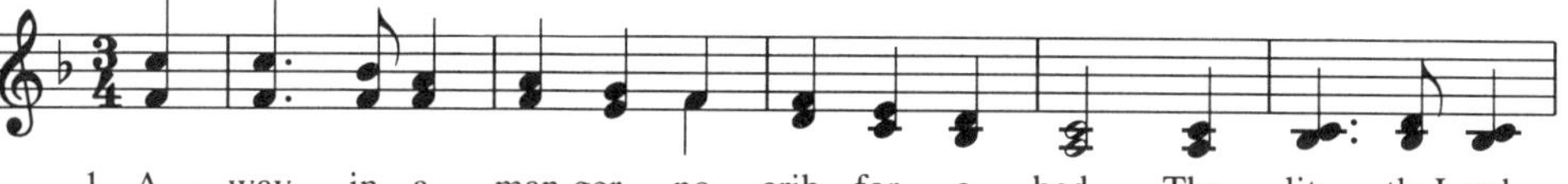

1. A - way in a man-ger, no crib for a bed, The lit - tle Lord
2. The cat - tle are low-ing, the Ba - by a - wakes, But lit - tle Lord
3. Be near me, Lord Je - sus, I ask thee to stay Close by me for

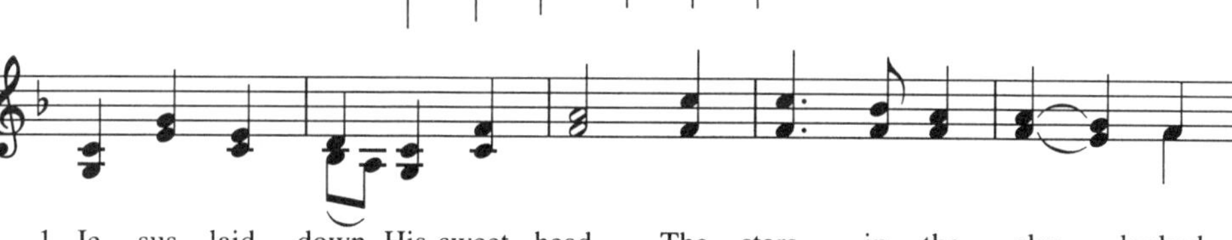

1. Je - sus laid down His sweet head. The stars in the sky looked
2. Je - sus, no cry - ing He makes, I love thee, Lord Je - sus, Look
3. ev - er, and love me, I pray. Bless all the dear chil - dren in

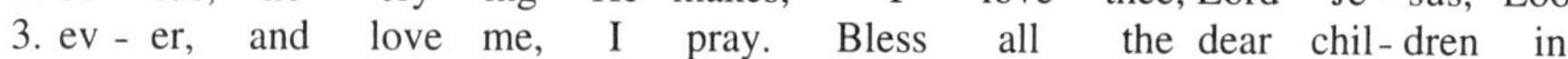

1. down where He lay, The lit - tle Lord Je - sus a - sleep on the hay.
2. down from the sky, And stay by my cra - dle till morn-ing is nigh.
3. thy ten - der care, And fit us for heav - en to live with thee there.

Words: Anonymous
Music: James R. Murray (1841-1905); arr. Edythe Ethelynn Woodruff (b. 1970). Used by Permission.

28 Down at the Cross

1. Down at the cross where my Sav - ior died, Down where for cleans - ing from
2. I am so won - drous - ly saved from sin, Je - sus so sweet - ly a -
3. O, pre - cious foun - tain that saves from sin, I am so glad I have
4. Come to this foun - tain so rich and sweet; Cast your poor soul at the

1. sin I cried; There to my heart was the blood ap - plied;
2. bides with - in; There at the cross where He took me in;
3. en - tered in; There Je - sus saves me and keeps me clean;
4. Sav - ior's feet; Plunge in to - day, and be made com - plete;

Glo - ry to His name. Glo - ry to His name. Glo - ry to His name!

There to my heart was the blood ap - plied; Glo - ry to His name.

Words: Elisha A. Hoffman (1839-1929)
Music: John H. Stockton (1813-1877)

Near the Cross

1. Je - sus, keep me near the cross, There's a pre - cious foun - tain;
2. Near the cross, a trem - bling soul, Love and mer - cy found me;
3. Near the cross! O Lamb of God, Bring its scenes be - fore me;
4. Near the cross. I'll watch and wait, Hop - ing, trust - ing ev - er,
1. Free to all, a heal - ing stream Flows from Cal - v'ry's moun - tain.
2. There the Bright and Morn - ing Star Sheds its beams a - round me.
3. Help me walk from day to day With its shad - ows o'er me.
4. Till I reach the gold - en strand Just be - yond the riv - er.
In the cross, in the cross Be my glo - ry ev - er;
Till my rap - tured soul shall find Rest be - yond the riv - er.

Words: Fanny J. Crosby (1820-1915)
Music: William H. Doane (1832-1915)

1. A - las! and did my Sav - ior bleed, and
2. Was it for crimes that I have done, He
3. Well might the sun in dark - ness hide, and
4. Thus might I hide my blush - ing face while
5. But drops of tears can ne'er re - pay the
1. did my Sov' - reign die? Would He de - vote that
2. groaned up - on the tree? A - maz - ing pit - y!
3. shut its glo - ries in; when God, the might - y
4. His dear cross ap - pears; dis - solve my heart in
5. debt of love I owe; Here, Lord, I give my -
1. sa - cred head for sin - ners such as I?
2. Grace un-known! And love be - yond de - gree!
3. mak - er, died for His own crea - ture's sin.
4. thank - ful-ness, and melt mine eyes to tears.
5. self a - way; 'tis all that I can do.
At the cross, at the cross, where I first __ saw the light, and the
bur-den of my heart rolled a-way; it was there by faith I re -

Words: Isaac Watts, 1707; refrain Ralph E. Hudson, 1885
Music: Ralph E. Hudson, 1885

ceived my sight, and now I am hap-py all the day.
Lead Me to Calvary
31
1. King of my life I crown thee now, Thine shall the glo-ry be;
2. Show me the tomb where thou wast laid, Ten-der-ly mourned and wept;
3. Let me, like Ma-ry, through the gloom, Come with a gift to thee;
4. May I be will-ing, Lord, to bear Dai-ly my cross for thee;
1. Lest I for-get thy thorn-crowned brow, Lead me to Cal-va-ry.
2. An-gels in robes of light ar-rayed Guard-ed thee whilst Thou slept.
3. Show to me now the emp-ty tomb,- Lead me to Cal-va-ry.
4. E-ven thy cup of grief to share- Thou hast borne all for me.
Lest I for-get Geth-sem-a-ne, Lest I for-get thine ag-o-ny,
Lest I for-get thy love for me, Lead me to Cal-va-ry.

Words: Jennie Evelyn Hussey (1874-1958)
Music: William J. Kirkpatrick (1838-1921)

Cal - va - ry, Cal - va - ry, Cal - va -
ry, Cal - va - ry, Cal - va - ry,
Cal - va - ry, Sure - ly He died on Cal - va - ry.
Fine
1. Ev - 'ry time I think a-bout Je - sus, Ev - 'ry time I
2. Don't you hear the ham - mer ring - ing, Don't you hear the
1. think a-bout Je - sus, Ev - ry time I think a - bout Je - sus,
2. ham - mer ring - ing, Don't you hear the ham - mer ring-ing,

Words: Traditional
Music: Negro Spiritual; arr. Carl Haywood (b. 1949), from *The Haywood Collection of Negro Spirituals*,

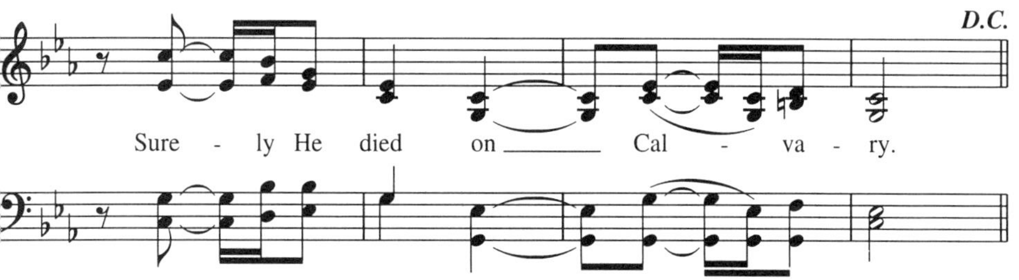
D.C.
Sure - ly He died on ___ Cal - va - ry.

3. Don't you hear Him calling His Father? Surely He died on Calvary.
4. Don't you hear Him say, "It is finished." Surely He died on Calvary.
5. Jesus furnished my salvation. Surely He died on Calvary.
6. Sinner do you love my Jesus? Surely He died on Calvary.

He Never Said a Mumbalin' Word 33

1. They cru - ci - fied_ my Lord, ___ and He nev - er said a mum-ba- lin'
2. They nailed Him to___ a tree, ___ and He nev - er said a mum-ba- lin'

1. word; They cru - ci - fied_ my Lord, ___ and He nev - er said a mum-ba- lin'
2. word; They nailed Him to ___ a tree, ___ and He nev - er said a mum-ba- lin'

1. word. Not a word, ___ not a word, ___ not a word.
2. word. Not a word, ___ not a word, ___ not a word.

3. They pierced Him in the side.
4. The blood came streamin' down.
5. He hung His head and died.

Words: Traditional
Music: Negro Spiritual; arr. Carl Haywood (b. 1949), from *The Haywood Collection of Negro Spirituals*,
Copyright © 1992.

He Will Remember Me

1. When on the cross of Cal-v'ry The Lord was cru - ci - fied;
2. O what a shame to kill Him There on that rug - ged cross;
3. At His dear feet I'm kneel-ing. My sins I now con - fess;
1. The mob stood 'round a - bout Him And mocked un - til He died.
2. But such a death was need - ed To res - cue all the lost.
3. I bow in deep re - pent-ance, My soul He'll sure - ly bless.
1. Two thieves were nailed be - side Him To share the ag - o - ny,
2. His blood was made a ran - som To set the cap - tives free,
3. My blind - ed eyes He o - pens So that the light I see,
1. But one of them cried out to Him, "O Lord, re-mem-ber me."
2. I know that I'm in - clud-ed, and He will re-mem-ber me.
3. And when I reach the pearl - y gates, He will re-mem-ber me.

Words: E. M. Bartlett (1885-1941)
Music: E. M. Bartlett

Will the Lord re - mem - ber me, When I am called to
Will the Lord re - mem - ber me,
go? When I have crossed death's chill - y sea, Will
When I have crossed death's chill - y sea,
He His love there show O yes, He heard my
yes, He heard my
fee - ble cries, From bond - age set me free. And
when I reach the pearl - y gates He will re - mem - ber me.

O How He Loves You and Me

1. O how He loves you and me.
2. Je - sus to Cal - vary did go,
1. O how He loves you and me;
2. His love for the worlds to show;
1. He gave His life, what more could He give;
2. What He did there brought hope from de - spair;
1. O how He loves you, O how He loves me,
2. O how He loves you, O how He loves me,
1. O how He loves you and me.
2. O how He loves you and me.

Words: Kurt Kaiser (b. 1934)
Music: Kurt Kaiser

O Sacred Head, Sore Wounded

1. O sa - cred head, sore wound - ed,
2. Thy beau - ty, long de - sir - ed,
3. In thy most bit - ter pas - sion
4. What lan - guage shall I bor - row
5. My days are few, O fail not,
1. de - filed and put to scorn;
2. hath van - ished from our sight;
3. my heart to share doth cry,
4. to thank thee, dear - est friend,
5. with thine im - mor - tal power,
1. O king - ly head. sur -
2. thy power is all ex -
3. with thee for my sal -
4. for this thy dy - ing
5. to hold me that I

ords: Paulus Gerhard (1607-1676)
usic: David Hurd (b. 1950)

1. round - ed with mock - ing
2. pir - ed, and quenched the
3. va - tion up - on the
4. sor - row, thy pit - y
5. quail not in death's most
1. crown of thorn; what
2. light of light. Ah
3. cross to die. Ah,
4. with - out end? Oh,
5. fear - ful hour; that
1. sor - row mars thy grand - eur? Can
2. me! for whom thou di - est, hide
3. keep my heart thus mov - ed to
4. make me thine for - ev - er! and
5. I may fight be - friend - ed, and

1. death thy bloom de - flower?
2. not so far thy grace,
3. stand thy cross be - neath,
4. should I faint - ing be,
5. see in my last strife
1. O coun - ten - ance whose splen - dor
2. show me, O Love most high - est,
3. to mourn thee, well - be - lov - ed,
4. Lord, let me nev - er, nev - er,
5. to me thine arms ex - tend - ed
1. the hosts of heav'n a - dore!
2. the bright - ness of thy face.
3. yet thank thee for thy death.
4. out - live my love for thee.
5. up - on the cross of life.

Were You There?

1. Were you there when they cru - ci - fied my Lord? Were you
2. Were you there when they nailed Him to the tree? Were you
3. Were you there when they laid Him in the tomb? Were you
4. Were you there when He rose up from the grave? Were you
1. there when they cru - ci - fied my Lord?
2. there when they nailed Him to the tree?
3. there when they laid Him in the tomb?
4. there when He rose up from the grave?
O!
Some - times it caus - es me to trem - ble, trem - ble, trem - ble.
1. Were you there when they cru - ci - fied my Lord?
2. Were you there when they nailed Him to the tree?
3. Were you there when they laid Him in the tomb?
4. Were you there when He rose up from the grave?

Words: Traditional
Music: Negro Spiritual; arr. Charles Winfred Douglas (1867-1944)

The Old Rugged Cross

1. On a hill far a - way stood an old rug - ged cross,
2. Oh, that old rug - ged cross so de - spised by the world,
3. In the old rug - ged cross, stained with blood so di - vine,
4. To the old rug - ged cross I will ev - er be true,
1. The em - blem of suf - f'ring and shame;
2. Has a won - drous at - trac - tion for me;
3. A won - drous beau - ty I see;
4. Its shame and re - proach glad - ly bear;
1. And I love that old cross where the dear - est and best
2. For the dear Lamb of God left His glo - ry a - bove,
3. For 'twas on that old cross Je - sus suf - fered and died,
4. Then He'll call me some day to my home far a - way,
1. For a world of lost sin - ners was slain.
2. To bear it to dark Cal - va - ry.
3. To par - don and sanc - ti - fy me.
4. Where His glo - ry for - ev - er I'll share.

Words: George Bennard (1873-1960)
Music: George Bennard

Hymn continues on the next page.

old rug - ged cross
So I'll cher - ish the cross, the old rug - ged cross,
Till my tro - phies at last I lay down;
old rug - ged cross,
I will cling to the cross, the old rug - ged cross,
And ex - change it some day for a crown.
39
There Is a Fountain
1. There is a foun - tain filled with blood Drawn
2. The dy - ing thief re - joiced to see That
3. Thou dy - ing Lamb, Thy pre - cious blood Shall
4. E'er since by faith I saw the stream Thy
5. Then in a no - bler, sweet - er song, I'll

1. from Im - man - uel's veins; And___ sin - ners, plunged be
2. foun - tain in___ his day; And___ there may I, though
3. nev - er lose___ its pow'r; Till___ all the ran - somed
4. flow - ing wounds_ sup - ply; Re - deem - ing love has
5. sing Thy pow'r___ to save; When___ this poor, lisp - ing
1. neath that flood, Lose___ all their guilt - y stains:___ Lose___
2. vile as he, Wash___ all my sins a - way:___ Wash___
3. Church of God Are___ saved, to sin no more:___ Are___
4. been my theme, And___ shall be till I die:___ And___
5. stamm - 'ring tongue Lies___ si - lent in the grave:___ Lies___
1. all their guilt - y stains,___ Lose all their guilt - y___ stains; And___
2. all my sins a - way,___ Wash all my sins_ a - way; And___
3. saved, to sin no more,___ Are saved, to sin_ no_ more; Till___
4. shall be till I die,___ And shall be till_ I___ die, Re -
5. si - lent in the grave,___ Lies si - lent in_ the_ grave; When_
1. sin - ners, plunged be - neath that flood, Lose_ all their guilt - y stains.
2. there may I, though vile as he, Wash_ all my sins a - way
3. all the ran - somed Church of God Are___ saved, to sin no more.
4. deem - ing love has been my theme, And___ shall be till I die.
5. this poor lisp - ing, stamm - 'ring tongue Lies___ si - lent in the grave.

Words: William Cowper (1731-1800)
Music: American Melody; arr. Lowell Mason (1792-1872)

40

He 'Ros

1. They cru - ci - fied my Sav - ior and nailed him to the tree, they cru - ci - fied my Sav - ior and nailed him to the tree, they cru - ci - fied my Sav - ior and nailed him to the tree, And the
2. Then Jo - seph begged his bod - y and laid it in the tomb, then Jo - seph begged his bod - y and laid it in the tomb, then Jo - seph begged his bod - y and laid it in the tomb, And the
3. Sis - ter Ma - ry, she came run - ning, a - look - ing for my Lord, Sis - ter Ma - ry, she came run - ning, a - look - ing for my Lord, Sis - ter Ma - ry, she came run - ning, a look - ing for my Lord, And the
4. An an - gel came from heav - en and rolled the stone a - way, an an - gel came from heav - en and rolled the stone a - way, an an - gel came from heav - en and rolled the stone a - way, And the

Words: Traditional
Music: Negro Spiritual; arr. William Farley Smith (b. 1941)

Lord will bear my spir - it home.
He 'rose, He 'rose, He 'rose _ from the dead! He
He 'rose He 'rose
'rose, He 'rose, He 'rose _ from the dead! He
He 'rose He 'rose
'rose, He 'rose, He 'rose _ from the dead, _ and the
He 'rose He 'rose
Lord will bear ______ my spir - it home.

Christ Has Arisen

Christ has a - ris - en, Al - le - lu - ia. Re - joice and
praise Him, Al - le - lu - ia. For our Re - deem - er burst from the
tomb, E - ven from death dis - pel - ling its gloom. Let us sing praise to Him
with end - less joy. Death's fear - ful sting He has come to de - stroy, Our sin for
giv - ing, Al - le - lu - ia. Je - sus is liv - ing, Al - le - lu - ia.

Words: Swahili Text; tr. Howard Olson
Music: Haya Tune; *Tumshandilie Mungu*, Makumira, Tanzania; harm. Carl Haywood (b. 1949), from *Songs of Praise*,

Ie Lives

1. I serve a ris - en Sav - ior, He's in the world to - day;
2. In all the world a - round me I see His lov - ing care,
3. Re - joice, re - joice. O Chris - tian, lift up your voice and sing.
1. I know that He is liv - ing, what - ev - er oth - ers say;
2. And though my heart grows wea - ry I nev - er will de - spair;
3. E - ter - nal hal - le - lu - jahs to Je - sus Christ, the King!
1. I see His hand of mer - cy, I hear His voice of cheer,
2. I know that He is lead - ing through all the storm - y blast,
3. The hope of all who seek Him, the help of all who find,
1. And just the time I need Him He's al - ways near.
2. The day of His ap - pear - ing will come at last.
3. None oth - er is so lov - ing, so good and kind.

/ords: Alfred H. Ackley (1887-1960)
Iusic: Alfred H. Ackley

He lives, He lives, Christ Je - sus lives to - day!
He lives, He lives,
He walks with me and talks with me a - long life's nar - row way.
He lives, He lives, sal - va - tion to im - part!
He lives, He lives,
You ask me how I know He lives? He lives with - in my heart.
43
Because He Live
1. God sent His Son, they called Him Je - sus; He came to love,
2. How sweet to hold a new-born ba - by, And feel the pride,
3. And then one day I'll cross the riv - er; I'll fight life's fi -

1. heal, and for - give; He lived and died to buy my
2. and joy he gives; But great-er still the calm as -
3. - nal war with pain; And then as death gives way to
1. par - don, An emp - ty grave is there to prove my Sav - ior lives.
2. sur - rance, This child can face un - cer - tain days be - cause He lives.
3. vic - t'ry, I'll see the lights of glo - ry and I'll know He lives.
Be - cause He lives I can face to - mo - row; Be - cause He lives
all fear is gone; Be - cause I know He holds the
fu - ture, And life is worth the liv - ing just be - cause He lives.

Words: Gloria Gaither (b. 1942) and William Gaither (b. 1936)
Music: William Gaither (b. 1936)

44 Blessed Absalom

(February 1

1. Born in bond-age, born in shack - les, Born stripped of all dig - ni - ty,
2. Seek - ing to ex - pand hor - i - zons, Bi - ble, pri - mer he did find;
3. When in Phi - la - del - phia set - tled, He sought per - sons in great need,
4. One fine morn - ing, while at wor - ship, Wrested from his knees in pray - er;
1. Abs'-lom Jones was bound, de - ter - mined, That he would one day be free.
2. To each word he was at - ten - tive, Learn - ing, lest he fall be - hind.
3. Ded - i - ca - ted to em - pow'r - ment, His own peo - ple did he lead.
4. He, his friends, were thus e - vic - ted: "You no more may praise God here."
1. Bless - ed Abs' - lom, leads us, guides us, In the bonds of u - ni - ty.
2. Bless - ed Abs' - lom, lib - er - ates us From the pri - son of our mind.
3. Bless - ed Abs' - lom, pray that we from All in - diff' - rence may be freed.
4. Bless - ed Abs' - lom, pray that we may Stand stead - fast and per - se - vere.

5. Founded he Saint Thomas' Church for
   Afric's sons and daughters blest;
   Full-fledged members of Christ's Body,
   They no longer were oppressed.
      Blessed Abs'lom, pray that we may
      Be the church at Christ's behest.

6. Blessed Abs'lom Jones, first priest of
   Afric's stock within our fold;
   May we, inspired by your witness
   Raise up priests with hearts of gold!
      Blessed Abs'lom, pioneer, prophet
      May your story long be told!

7. Praise to Christ the Liberator;
   Praise Creator ever blest;
   Praise the Spirit, Source of comfort
   North to south, and east to west:
      Blessed Abs'lom, priest, exemplar,
      In God's bosom now at rest.

Words: Harold T. Lewis (b. 1947)
Music: *Lauda Anima*, John Goss (1800-1880)

Augustine of Hippo

(August 28 or May 5)

1. O Mon - i - ca, blest mo - ther, A well of ho - ly tears; For
2. But Je - sus, Word In - car - nate Re - vealed to him the Truth; Aug -
3. Re - turned to his own home - land, As - sumed he Hip - po's see; Staunch
4. Aug - us - tine, faith - ful bi - shop, Con - fes - sor to the end, In -
1. thy dear son, Au - gus - tine, You shed for ma - ny years. That
2. gus - tine, thus con - vert - ed, For - sook his way - ward youth. Re -
3. cham - pion of the faith, He fought each her - e - sy. He
4. flame our hearts with pas - sion For Je - sus, Lord and Friend. Au -
1. he might learn the faith that the Lord's A - pos - tles taught, But
2. nounc - ing Sa - tan's cun - ning, Pre - vailed he in that hour; And
3. taught the Church is ho - ly, Though sin - ners do a - bound; That
4. gus - tine, ho - ly doc - tor, Thou son of Af - ric's sod, Help
1. far from Af - ric's coast, strange Phi - los - o - phies he sought.
2. at the hands of Am - brose Re - ceived bap - ti - sm's pow'r.
3. in gifts sa - cra - ment - al Is true grace to be found.
4. us to reach the gates of The Ci - ty of our God.

Words: Harold T. Lewis (b. 1947), Copyright © 1992.
Music: Marvin Curtis (b. 1951), Copyright © 1991

Blessed Martin, Pastor, Prophe

(January 15 or April 4

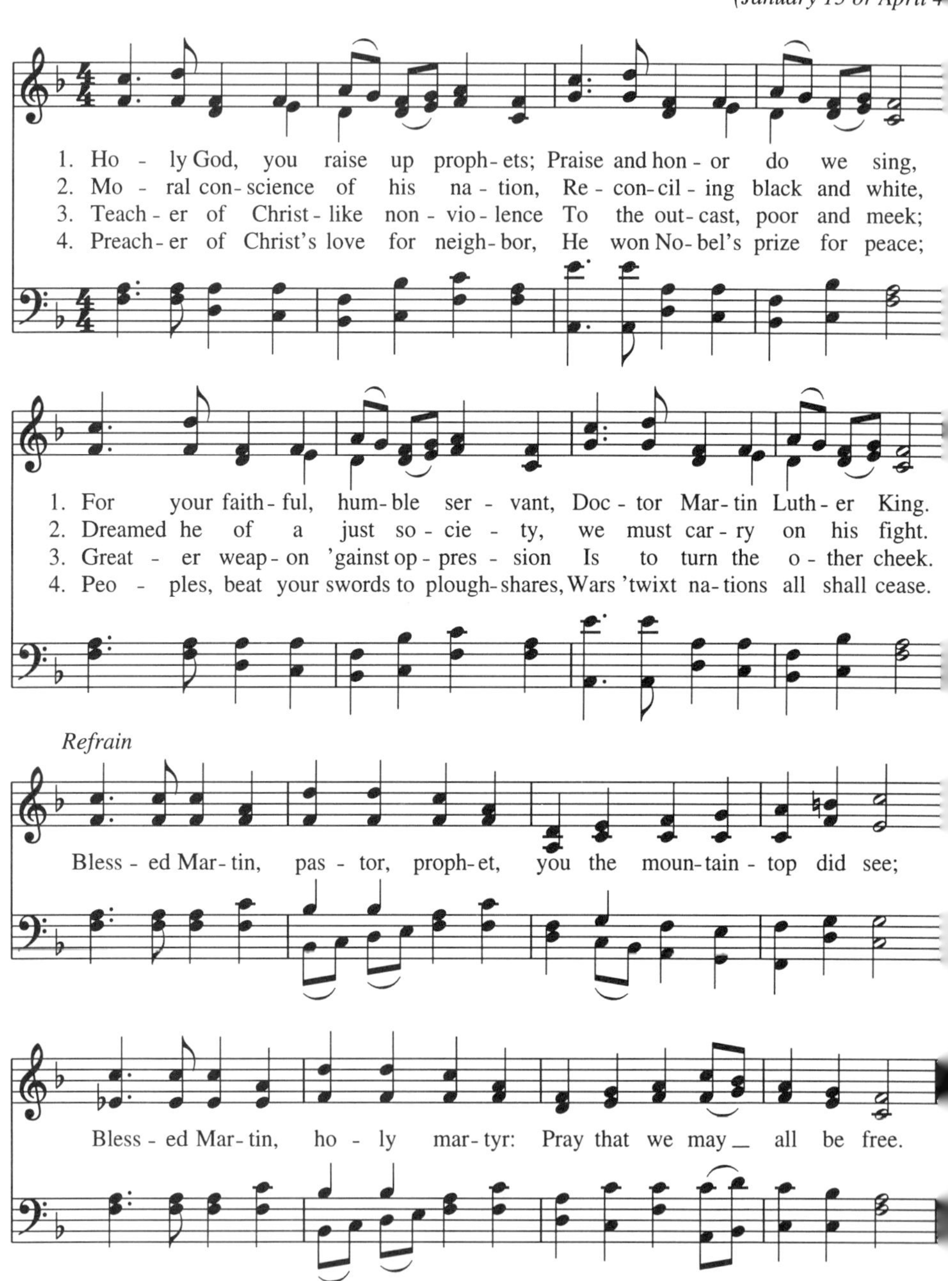
1. Ho - ly God, you raise up proph - ets; Praise and hon - or do we sing,
2. Mo - ral con - science of his na - tion, Re - con - cil - ing black and white,
3. Teach - er of Christ - like non - vio - lence To the out - cast, poor and meek;
4. Preach - er of Christ's love for neigh - bor, He won No - bel's prize for peace;
1. For your faith - ful, hum - ble ser - vant, Doc - tor Mar - tin Luth - er King.
2. Dreamed he of a just so - cie - ty, we must car - ry on his fight.
3. Great - er weap - on 'gainst op - pres - sion Is to turn the o - ther cheek.
4. Peo - ples, beat your swords to plough - shares, Wars 'twixt na - tions all shall cease.
Refrain
Bless - ed Mar - tin, pas - tor, proph - et, you the moun - tain - top did see;
Bless - ed Mar - tin, ho - ly mar - tyr: Pray that we may _ all be free.

5. Champion of oppressed humanity
Suff'ring throughout all the world;
He offered pride and dignity
Let Christ's banner be unfurled!
Refrain

6. So, when felled by sniper's bullet,
Under heavens overcast,
He could cry, "Thank God Almighty,
I am free, I'm free at last!"
Refrain

Words: Harold T. Lewis (b. 1947), Copyright © 1992
Music: *Martin's Song* by Carl Haywood (b. 1949), from *Songs of Praise*, Copyright © 1992

Cyprian of Carthage

(September 13)

1. O Cyp - ri - an, con - vert to the faith, Made bish - op
2. O Cyp - ri - an, you did teach that we who God Al -
3. O Cyp - ri - an, you did teach that we out - side the
4. Stead - fast de - fend - er of the truth, through Af - ric's
1. of the Car - thage See, Be - set, by schism,
2. might - y Fa - ther call, Must claim the church, The
3. church can - not be saved, Help us to bring forth
4. coast you gained re - nown, Who per - se - cu - ted,
1. war and strife, Preached to the faith - ful u - ni - ty.
2. Bride of Christ As the true moth - er of us all.
3. pen - i - tents Un - to Christ's font, that they be laved.
4. and be - sieged, Re - ceived, at last, the mar - tyr's crown.

5. O Cyprian bishop, martyr blest
Pray for us at God's heav'nly throne,
That we, who Christ's true faith confess
May Father, Son and Spirit own.

Words: Harold T. Lewis (b. 1947)
Music: *Rockingham*, from Second Supplement to Psalmody in Miniature, c. 1780; harm. Edward Miller (1731-1807)

Blessed Monica

(May 4)

1. In Af - ric's north- ern coast - land When Moth - er Church was young,
2. Ex - em - plar for all moth - ers, And pat - ron saint of wives,
3. Saint Mo - ni - ca en - treat - ed The throne of heav'n - ly grace,
4. In Os - tia's port, Au - gus - tine Heard her last dy - ing word;
1. Was born the ho - ly wo - man Of whom this hymn is sung.
2. She led her spouse and child - ren In ho - ly, Christ- ian lives.
3. That her dear son, Au - gus - tine The Gos - pel might em - brace.
4. He wished his moth- er's bo - dy In Af - ric's soil in - terred.
1. O Mon - i - ca, be - lov - ed be - fore God thee we own,
2. Af fec- tion, pa - tience, wis - dom, True zeal and con- stan - cy:
3. Her tear - ful prayers were an - swered, Her heart no long - er ri - ven;
4. "No place is far from God," Was her most ur - gent plea;
1. Our con - stant in - ter - ces - sor Be - fore His heav'n- ly throne.
2. With these gifts God en - dowed her And ho - ly Char - i - ty.
3. Con - fes - sor, bish - op, doc - tor She to the Church has giv'n.
4. "When at God's ho - ly al - tar Do there re - mem - ber me."

5. O Saint of perserverance
Be with us as we pray;
That we with zeal and ardor
Might serve our God alway:

To whom we raise our praises
As will be ever meet,
To Father, Son Eternal
And Holy Paraclete.

Words: Harold T. Lewis (b. 1947)
Music: *Lancashire*, Henry Thomas Smart (1813-1879)

Simon of Cyrene

(May 12) also suitable for Passiontide

1. O Je - sus scourged, de - rid - ed, mocked, up
2. The sol - diers spat u - pon His face, His
3. His strength gave out, He tried in vain, Gol -
4. He came up from Cy - re - ne When the
1. Cal - va-ry's hill did tread; But un - der - load of
2. rai - ment did they strip; And thus ex - posed to
3. go - tha to as - cend; And so it was that
4. sol - diers him did seize; He was com - pelled to
1. splin - t'ry wood He fell u - pon His head.
2. com - mon gaze He suf - fered 'neath the whip.
3. Si - mon blest Be - came our Lord's dear friend.
4. bear the cross and so Je - sus did please.

5. His muscular frame bore Christ's own Tree
Along the Sacred Way;
"O Jesus, who will die for me
I'll follow Thee alway."

6. O Simon, joyful crucifer
Before the throne of grace:
Pray that we who shall bear His cross
May see Him face to face.

The melody may be sung in canon at distances of either two or three beats.

Words: Harold T. Lewis (b. 1947), Copyright © 1992.
Music: *New Britain*, from *Virginia Harmony*, 1831; adapt. Edwin Othello Excell (1851-1921);
harm. Austin Cole Lovelace (b. 1919), Harm. Copyright © 1964 Abingdon Press

Philip the Evangelis

(October 1

1. The an - gel said to Phil - ip: "Go to a des - ert place."
2. The E - thi - ope re - spond - ed: "Lead me and be my guide."
3. They trav - elled in the char - iot, And came up - on a brook;
4. Saint Phil - lip told the E - thiope: "Be - lieve with all your heart;
1. And there he found an E - thiope, the treas - urer to Can - dace,
2. Ex - plain the scrip - ture to me; "Here, sit down at my side."
3. The E - thi - ope, ex - ci - ted then looked up from his book.
4. And God the Ho - ly Spir - it Will His own gift im - part."
1. Who sat with - in his char - iot with Ho - ly Writ in hand.
2. Then Phil - ip ex - e - ge - ted I - sai - ah's Ho - ly word.
3. "See Phil - ip, here is wa - ter," He said, and stopped his steed!
4. "I do be - lieve that Je - sus Is God's true, on - ly son."

Words: Harold T. Lewis (b. 1947), Copyright © 1992.
Music: *Nyland,* Finnish Folk Melody; adapt. David Evans (1874-1948)

1. Asked Phil - ip: "Can you,_ bro - ther, the Pro - phet un - der - stand?"
2. And preached un - to the _ E - thiope that Je - sus Christ is Lord.
3. "What can now," he im - plored him, "My bap - tism _____ im - pede?"
4. And with these words, the _ treas - urer A great - er__ treas - ure won.

5. O Philip, the evangelist
You brought to Afric's seed
The Gospel of our Savior
In thought, and word and deed,
O may we share Thy fervor
And press on towards the prize;
And heed our Lord's commission
To teach, preach and baptize.

alamu Maria

larch 25 or August 15)

51

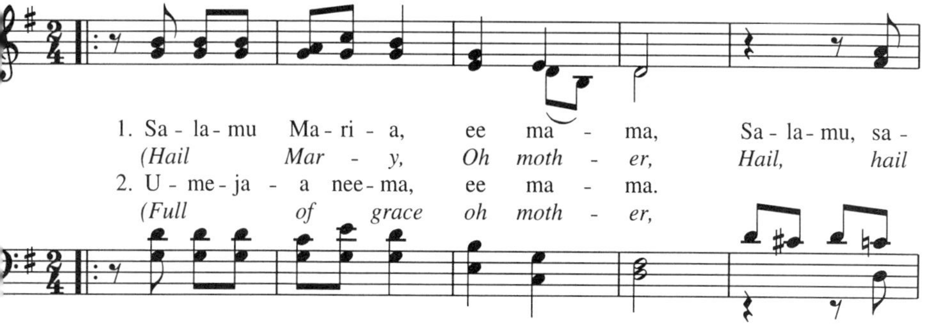
1. Sa - la - mu Ma - ri - a, ee ma - ma, Sa - la - mu, sa -
(Hail Mar - y, Oh moth - er, Hail, hail
2. U - me - ja - a nee - ma, ee ma - ma.
(Full of grace oh moth - er,

1.
2.
la - mu Ma - ri - a, Ma - ri - a; ri - a.
Mar - y, Mar - y; y.)

ords: African Folk Hymn
isic: African Melody

52

God Has Smiled on Me

God has smiled on me,
He has set me free.
God has smiled on me,
He's been good to me.

Words: Isaiah Jones
Music: Isaiah Jones; refrain harm. Hezekiah Brinson, Jr. (b. 1958)

1.
2.
Fine
1. He is the source of all
2. A light unto my path
1.
2.
Fine
1. my joy, He fills me with His love The grace
2. is He, my strength when I would fall He guides
D.C.
1. that I employ, He sends: down from a-bove.
2. each day for me, God is my all and all.

Expression of Life

Glo - ry to God in the high - est, He is the might - y
King, Mas - ter of ever - y thing, The cap - tain of my soul, The u - ni -
verse con - trol, God is the one true ex - pres - sion of life.
He's the cre - a - tor, A great cre - a - tor,
Hea - ven and earth His great - ness pro - claim.
The cap - tain of my soul, The u - ni verse con - trol,

Words: Turner Hughes
Music: Frank E. White

Ho - nor and ma - jes - ty se - cond to none.
Nearer, My God, to Thee
54
1. Near - er, my God, to Thee, Near - er to Thee!
2. Though like the wan - der - er, The sun goes down,
3. There let the way ap - pear, Steps un - to heav'n;
4. Then, with my wak - ing thoughts, Bright with Thy praise,
5. Or if on joy - ful wing, Cleav - ing the sky,
1. E'en though it be a cross That rais - eth me;
2. Dark - ness be o - ver me, My rest a stone;
3. All that Thou send - est me, In mer - cy giv'n;
4. Out of my ston - y griefs, Beth - el I'll raise;
5. Sun, moon and stars for - got, Up - wards I fly,
1. Still all my song would be
2. Yet in my dreams I'd be
3. An - gels to beck - on me Near - er, my God, to Thee,
4. So by my woes to be
5. Still all my song shall be
Near - er my God, to Thee, Near - er to Thee.

Words: Sarah F. Adams (1805-1848)
Music: Bethany, Lowell Mason (1792-1872)

1. In God we trust, with all our heart and soul, In God we trust to reach our righ - teous goal, En - shrined in Thee for - ev - er may we be, Come what may, Keep faith and pray, in God we trust, in
(2. In) God we trust, wher - ev - er we may roam, In God we trust to bless our land and home, Through all our days we'll al - ways sing His praise, Come what may, Our hearts will pray, in God we trust, in
God we trust
God we trust,

Words: Anonymous
Music: Anonymous; arr. C. Julian Parrish (b. 1911)
Folks year round worship song, arranged for use in hymnals and supplements to hymnals by C. Julian Parrish.

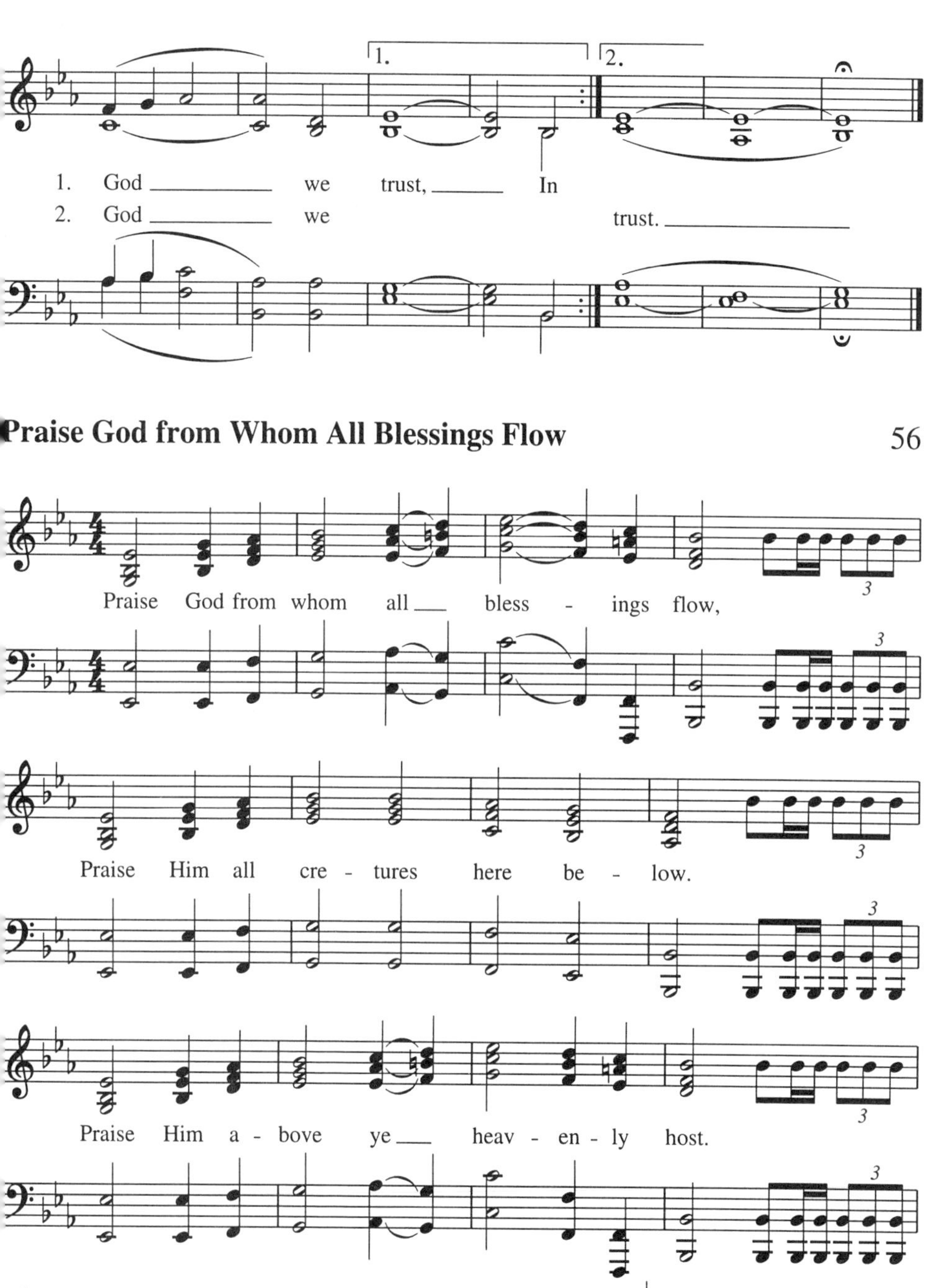
1.
2.
1. God we trust, In
2. God we trust.
Praise God from whom all bless - ings flow,
3
Praise Him all cre - tures here be - low.
3
Praise Him a - bove ye heav - en - ly host.
3

Praise God from Whom All Blessings Flow 56

Praise Fa - ther, Son and Ho - ly Ghost.

Words: Isaac Watts (1675-1748); and William Keathe (d. 1593); adapt. Thomas Ken (1637-1711)
Music: John Hatton (d. 1793); adapt. George Coles; harm. Roberta Martin (1912-1969)

Oh Lord, How Perfect Is Your Name

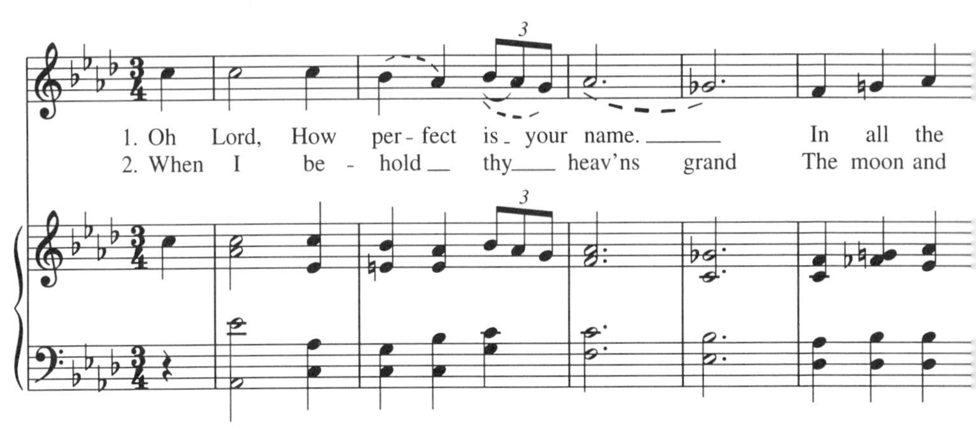
1. Oh Lord, How per - fect is your name. In all the
2. When I be - hold thy heav'ns grand The moon and

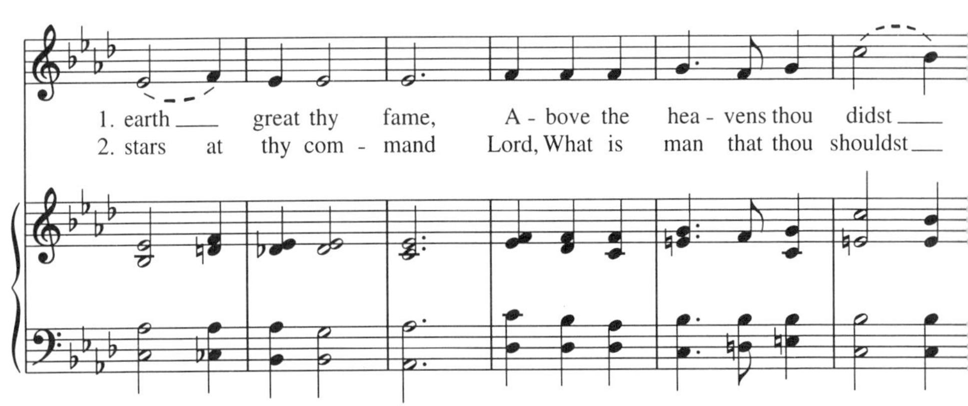
1. earth great thy fame, A - bove the hea - vens thou didst
2. stars at thy com - mand Lord, What is man that thou shouldst

1. set Thy glo - ry gra - cious Lord, and yet out of the mouths of babes calls
2. heed his call or vi - sit his seed, Near an - gels then have fixed stead -

Words: Hymn Tune
Music: Irma Tillery (b. 1925). Used by Permission.

1. Thee, Thy strength to ___ still the ___ en - e - my!
2. fast the ho - nor ___ and glo-ry crown His head.

The Lord Is My Light 58

The Lord is my light and my sal - va - tion, the Lord is my light and my sal - va - tion, the Lord is my light and my sal - va - tion; whom shall I ___ fear?

Hymn continues on the next page.

Words: Lillian Bouknight
Music: Lillian Bouknight; arr. Paul Gainer

Whom shall I fear, whom shall I fear?
The Lord is the strength of my life;
whom shall I fear? In the time of trou - ble,
He shall hide me, O in the time of trou - ble,
He shall hide me, in the time of trou - ble,
He shall hide me; whom shall I fear?

1. I trust in God wher - ev - er I may be, Up - on the
2. He makes the rose an ob - ject of His care, He guides the
3. I trust in God, for, in the li - on's den, On bat - tle -
4. The val - ley may be dark, the sha - dows deep, But oh, the
1. land or on the roll - ing sea; For come what
2. ea - gle through the path - less air; And sure - ly
3. field, or in the pris - on pen; Through praise or
4. shep - herd guards His lone - ly sheep; And through the
1. may, from day to day,
2. He re - mem - bers me,
3. blame, through flood or flame,
4. gloom, He'll lead me home,
My heav'n - ly Fa - ther watch - es o - ver
me. I trust in God, I know He cares for me, On moun - tain

Hymn continues on the next page.

Vords: W. C. Martin
Iusic: Charles H. Gabriel (1856-1932); arr. J. Jefferson Cleveland (1937-1988) and Verolga Nix (b. 1933)

bleak or on the storm-y sea; Though bil-lows roll, He keeps my

soul, My heav'n-ly Fa-ther watch-es o-ver me.

60 How Great Thou Art

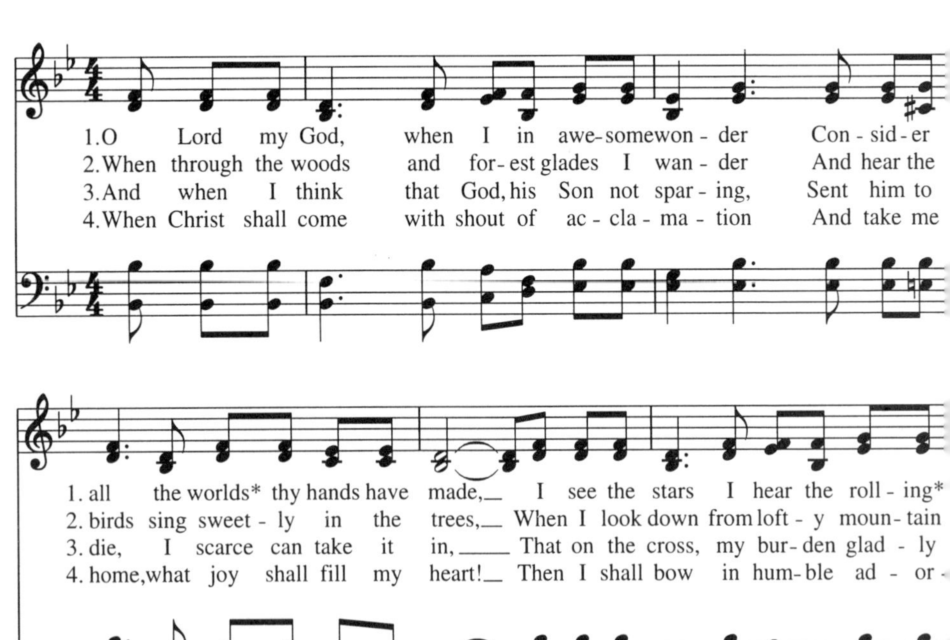
1. O Lord my God, when I in awe-some won-der Con-sid-er
2. When through the woods and for-est glades I wan-der And hear the
3. And when I think that God, his Son not spar-ing, Sent him to
4. When Christ shall come with shout of ac-cla-ma-tion And take me
1. all the worlds* thy hands have made, I see the stars I hear the roll-ing*
2. birds sing sweet-ly in the trees, When I look down from loft-y moun-tain
3. die, I scarce can take it in, That on the cross, my bur-den glad-ly
4. home, what joy shall fill my heart! Then I shall bow in hum-ble ad-or-

* *The translator's original words are "works" and "mighty."*

Words: Stuart K. Hine (1899-1989)
Music: Swedish Folk Melody; arr. Stuart K. Hine

1. thun - der, Thy pow'r through - out the u - ni - verse dis - played.
2. gran - deur, And hear the brook and feel the gen - tle breeze.
3. bear - ing, He bled and died to take a - way my sin.
4. ra - tion, And there pro - claim, my God, how great thou art.
Then sings my soul, my Sav - ior, God, to Thee; How great Thou
art, how great Thou art! Then sings my soul, my Sav - ior God, to
Thee: How great Thou art, how great Thou art!

61 The Right Hand of God

1. The right hand of God is writ-ing in our land,
2. The right hand of God is point-ing in our land,
3. The right hand of God is strik-ing in our land,
4. The right hand of God is heal-ing in our land,
5. The right hand of God is plant-ing in our land,
1. Writ - ing with pow - er and with love,
2. Point - ing the way we must go.
3. Strik-ing out at en - vy, hate, and greed.
4. Heal-ing bro - ken bod - ies, minds, and souls.
5. Plant-ing seeds of free - dom, hope, and love.
1. Our con-flicts and our fears, our tri-umphs and our
2. So cloud - ed is the way, so eas - i - ly we
3. Our sel - fish - ness and lust, our pride and deeds un -
4. So won-drous is its touch with love that means so
5. In these Ca - rib - bean lands, let His peo-ple all join
1. tears Are re - cord - ed by the right hand of God.
2. stray, But we're guid-ed by the right hand of God.
3. just Are de - stroyed by the right hand of God.
4. much, When we're healed by the right hand of God.
5. hands, And be one by the right hand of God.

Words: Patrick Prescod
Music: Noel Dexter

JESUS CHRIST OUR LORD

In Christ There Is No East or West

62

1. In ___ Christ there is no ___ East or West, In
2. In ___ Him shall true hearts ev - ery - where Their
3. Join ___ hands, di - ci - ples of the faith, What
4. In ___ Christ now meet both East and West, In

1. Him no South or ___ North; ___ But ___ one great fel - low -
2. high com - mu - nion ___ find; ___ His ___ ser - vice is the
3. e'er your race may ___ be! ___ Who ___ serves my Fa - ther
4. Him meet South and ___ North; ___ All ___ Christ - ly souls are

1. ship of love Through - out the whole wide earth.
2. gold - en cord Close - bind - ing hu - man kind.
3. as a son Is sure - ly kin to me.
4. one in him Through out the whole wide earth.

Words: Galatians 3:28; adapt. John Oxenham (1852-1941)
Music: *McKee*, Negro Spiritual; adapt. Harry T. Burleigh (1866-1949)

Glorious is the Name of Jesus

Glo - rious is the Name of Je - sus, Prais - es to His
Name. Oh, glo - rious and right - eous and
Ho - ly is His Name. Oh, glo - ri - ous is His
Name. I feel His pres - ence

Words: Robert J. Fryson
Music: Robert J. Fryson

in this place, His Spir - it has con - trol, Can't you
feel His warm em - brace and all the joy with - in your
soul, Oh, glo - ri - ous is His
Name, Oh, glo - ri - ous is His Name.

I Love To Tell the Story

1. I love to tell the sto - ry Of un - seen things a - bove,
2. I love to tell the sto - ry, For those who know it best
1. Of Je - sus and His glo - ry, Of Je - sus and His love.
2. Seem hun - ger-ing and thirst - ing To hear it, like the rest.
1. I love to tell the sto - ry, Be - cause I know it's true;
2. And when, in scenes of glo - ry, I sing the new, new song,
1. It sat - is - fies my long - ings As noth - ing else would do.
2. 'Twill be the old, old sto - ry That I have loved so long.
I love to tell the sto - ry; 'Twill be my theme in glo - ry.

Words: A. Katherine Hankey (1831-1911)
Music: William G. Fischer (1835-1912)

To tell the old, old sto - ry Of Je - sus and His love.
Bless The Lord, O My Soul
65
Bless the Lord, O my soul: and all that is with -
in me, Bless His ho - ly name.
Fine
He has done great things, He has done great
things, He has done great things, Bless His ho - ly name!
D.C.

Words: Psalm 103:1
Music: Andrae Crouch (b. 1942)

I Must Tell Jesus

1. I must tell Je - sus all of my tri - als; I can - not bear these burdens a - lone, In my dis - tress He kind - ly will help me, He ev - er loves and cares for His own.
2. I must tell Je - sus all of my trou - bles, He is a kind, com - pas - sion - ate friend; If I but ask Him, He will de - liv - er, Make of my trou - bles quick - ly an end.
3. Tempt - ed and tried I need a great Sav - ior, One who can help my bur - dens to bear; I must tell Je - sus, I must tell Je - sus; He all my cares and sor - rows will share.
4. O how the world to e - vil al - lures me! O how my heart is tempt - ed to sin! I must tell Je - sus, and He will help me, O - ver the world the vic - t'ry to win.
I must tell Je - sus! I must tell Je - sus! I can - not bear my bur - dens a - lone; I must tell Je - sus! I must tell

Words: Elisha A. Hoffman (1839-1929)
Music: Elisha A. Hoffman

Je - sus! Je - sus can help me, Je - sus a - lone.
Love the Lord
67
1. I love the Lord, He heard my
2. I love the Lord, He heard my
1. cry and pit - ied ev - 'ry groan.
2. cry and pit - ied ev - 'ry groan.
1. Long as I live and trou - bles rise,
2. O let my heart no more des - pair
1. I'll has - ten to His throne.
2. while I have breath to pray.

Words: Traditional
Music: Traditional; arr. Richard Smallwood

I've Decided to Make Jesus My Choice

1. Some folk_ would_ rath - er ___ have __ hous - es ____ and land. ____
2. These clothes may be rag - ged __ that I'm wear - ing. _____
1. Some folk ____ choose sil - ver ____ and gold. ________
2. Heav - y ______ is the load that ____ I'm bear - ing ________
1.These things ____ they treas - ure _____ and for - get a-bout their
2.These old __________ bur - dens ____ that I'm car - -
1. soul;
2. rying
I've de - ci - ded ___ to make Je - sus my choice. ______

Words: Harris Johnson
Music: Harris Johnson

The road is rough, the go - ing gets tough, and the
hills are hard to climb, I've start - ed out a
long time a - go, there's no doubt in my mind; I've de -
cid - ed to make Je - sus my choice.

1. I come to the gar - den a - lone, While the
2. He speaks, and the sound of His voice Is so
3. I'd stay in the gar - den with Him Though the
1. dew is still on the ros - es; And the voice I hear, fall - ing
2. sweet the birds hush their sing - ing; And the me - lo - dy that He
3. night a - round me be fall - ing; But He bids me go through the
1. on my ear, The Son of God dis - clos - es.
2. gave to me With - in my heart is ring - ing.
3. voice of woe, His voice to me is call - ing.
And He walks with me, and He talks with me, And He
tells me I am His own, And the joy we share as we

Words: C. Austin Miles (1868-1946)
Music: C. Austin Miles

tar - ry there, None oth - er has ev - er ___ known. ___
1. I want Je - sus ___ to walk with me (walk with me); I want
2. In my tri - als, ___ Lord, walk with me (walk with me); In my
3. In my sor - rows, ___ Lord, walk with me (walk with me); In my
1. Je - sus ___ to walk _ with me (walk with me); All a
2. tri - als, ___ Lord, walk _ with me (walk with me); When the
3. sor - rows, ___ Lord, walk _ with me (walk with me); When my
1. long my ___ pil - grim jour - ney, ___ Lord, I want
2. shades of ___ life ___ are fall - ing, ___ Lord, I want
3. heart with - in ___ is ach - ing, ___ Lord, I want
1. Je - sus ___ to walk with me (walk with me).
2. Je - sus ___ to walk with me (walk with me).
3. Je - sus ___ to walk with me (walk with me).

Want Jesus to Walk with Me

70

Words: Traditional
Music: Negro Spiritual; arr. Carl Haywood (b. 1949), from *The Haywood Collection of Negro Spirituals*,

In Times Like Thes

1. In times like these you need a Savior, In times like these
2. In times like these you need the Bi - ble, In times like these
3. In times like these I have a Sav - ior, In times like these
1. you need an an - chor; Be ver - y sure, be ver - y sure.
2. O be not i - dle; Be ver - y sure, be ver - y sure.
3. I have an an - chor, I'm ver - y sure, I'm ver - y sure.
1. Your an-chor holds and grips the Sol - id Rock!
2. Your an-chor holds and grips the Sol - id Rock!
3. My an-chor holds and grips the Sol - id Rock!
This Rock is Je - sus, Yes, He's the One; This Rock is Je - sus,
The on - ly One! 1,2. Be ver - y sure, be ver - y sure
3. I'm ver - y sure, I'm ver - y sure

Words: Ruth Caye Jones (1902-1972)
Music: Ruth Caye Jones

1, 2. Your an - chor holds ___ and grips the Sol - id Rock! ___
3. My an - chor holds ___ and grips the Sol - id Rock! ___

ust a Closer Walk with Thee

72

1. I am weak but thou art strong; ___
2. Through this world of toil and snares, ___
3. When my fee - ble life is o'er, ___
Refrain: Just a clos - er walk with thee, ___

1. Je - sus, keep me from all wrong; ___ I'll be sat - is - fied as
2. If I fal - ter, Lord, who cares? ___ Who with me my bur-den
3. Time for me will be no more; ___ Guide me gent - ly, safe - ly
Refrain: Grant it, Je - sus, is my plea, ___ Dai - ly walk - ing close to

D.C. for Refrain
1. long ___ As I walk, let me walk close to thee.
2. shares? ___ None but thee, dear ___ Lord, none but thee.
3. o'er ___ To Thy king - dom ___ shore, to thy shore.
Refrain: thee, ___ Let it be, dear ___ Lord, let it be.

ords: Anonymous
lusic: American Folk Song

Is There Anybody Here Who Loves My Jesus?

Is there an - y - bod - y here who loves my Je - sus?
An - y - bod - y here who loves my Lord?
I want to know if you love my Je - sus;
I want to know if you love my Lord.
Fine
1. This world's a wil - der - ness of woe,
2. Re - li - gion is a bloom - ing rose,
3. When I was blind and could not see.
4. When ev - 'ry star re - fus - es to shine,
1. So let us all to glo - ry go.
2. And none but them who feel it know.
3. King Je - sus brought the light to me.
4. I know King Je - sus will be mine.
D.C

Words: Traditional
Music: Negro Spiritual

Je - su, Je - su, fill us with your love, show
us how to serve the neigh-bors we have from you.
Fine
1. Kneels at the feet of his friends, si - lent - ly wash-es their
2. Neigh-bors are rich and poor, neigh-bors are black and
3. These are the ones we should serve, these are the ones we should
4. Lov - ing puts us on our knees, serv - ing as though we are
5. Kneel at the feet of our friends, si - lent - ly wash-ing their
D.C.
1. feet, Mas - ter who acts as a slave to them.
2. white, neigh-bors are near and far a - way.
3. love; all these are neigh-bors to us and you.
4. slaves, this is the way we should live with you.
5. feet, this is the way we should live with you.

ords: John 13:1-17; adapt. Tom Colvin, 1969
usic: Ghana Folk Song; adapt. Tom Colvin, 1969; harm. Charles H. Webb, 1988

75 Jesu, Joy of Our Desirin

1. Je - su, Joy of our de - sir - ing, Ho - ly wis - dom love most bright.
2. This the way where hope is guid - ing, Hear what peace - ful mu - sic rings.
1. Drawn by thee our souls as - pir - ing, Soar to un - cre - a - ted light.
2. Where the flock in thee con - fi - ding, Drink of joy from breath - less springs.
1. Word of God our flesh that fash - ioned. With the fire of, life im - pas - sionec
2. Theirs is beau - ty's fair - est pleas - ure. Theirs is wis-doms ho - liest trea - sures.
1. Striv - ing still to truth un - known, Soar - ing, dy - ing 'round thy throne.
2. Thou dost ev - er lead thine own, In the love of joys un - known.

Words: Martin Janus
Music: William B. Cooper

Jesus in the Morning

76

1. Je - sus, Je - sus, Je - sus in the morn - ing
2. Praise Him, Praise Him, Praise Him in the morn - ing
3. Love Him, Love Him, Love Him in the morn - ing
4. Serve Him, Serve Him, Serve Him in the morn - ing
5. Je - sus, Je - sus, Je - sus in the morn - ing
1. Je - sus in the noon - time; Je - sus,
2. Praise Him in the noon - time; Praise Him,
3. Love Him in the noon - time; Love Him,
4. Serve Him in the noon - time; Serve Him,
5. Je - sus in the noon - time; Je - sus,
1. Je - sus, Je - sus when the sun goes down!
2. Praise Him, Praise Him when the sun goes down!
3. Love Him, Love Him when the sun goes down!
4. Serve Him, Serve Him when the sun goes down!
5. Je - sus, Je - sus when the sun goes down!

Words: Traditional
Music: Negro Spiritual

77

Jesus Is All the World to M

1. Je - sus is all the world to me. My life, my joy, my
2. Je - sus is all the world to me, My friend in tri - als
3. Je - sus is all the world to me, And true to Him I'll
4. Je - sus is all the world to me, I want no bet - ter
1. all; He is my strength from day to day, With
2. sore; I go to Him for bless - ings, and He
3. be; Oh, how could I this friend de - ny, When
4. friend; I trust Him now, I'll trust Him when Life's
1. out Him I would fall: When I am sad, to
2. gives them o'er and o'er; He sends the sun - shine
3. He's so true to me? Fol - low - ing Him I
4. fleet - ing days shall end: Beau - ti - ful life with
1. Him I go. No oth - er one can cheer me so;
2. and the rain. He sends the har - vest's gold - en grain;
3. know I'm right. He watch - es o'er me day and night;
4. such a friend. Beau - ti - ful life that has no end;

Words: Will L. Thompson (1847-1909)
Music: Will L. Thompson

1. When I am sad He makes me glad, He's my friend.
2. Sun - shine and rain, har - vest of grain, He's my friend.
3. Fol - low - ing Him by day and night, He's my friend.
4. E - ter - nal life, e - ter - nal joy, He's my friend.

Blessed Be the Name

78

1. Bless - ed be the name! Bless - ed be the name! Bless - ed be the name of the Lord! Bless - ed be the name! Bless - ed be the name! Bless - ed be the name of the Lord!

2. Jesus is the
name of the Lord!

3. Worthy to be grand
is the Lord!

Words: Psalm 72:19
Music: Campmeeting Melody; arr. Ralph E. Hudson, 1887

Jesus, Lover of My Sou

1. Je - sus, lov - er of my soul, Let me to thy bo - som fly,
2. Oth - er ref - uge have I none, Hangs my help - less soul on thee;
3. Plen - teous grace with thee is found, Grace to cleanse from ev - 'ry sin;
1. While the near - er wa - ters roll, While the tem - pest still is high;
2. Leave, ah! leave me not a - lone, Still sup - port and com - fort me!
3. Let the heal - ing streams a - bound, Make and keep me pure with - in.
1. Hide me, O my Sa - vior, hide, Till the storm of life be past;
2. All my trust on thee is stayed; All my help from thee I bring;
3. Thou of life the foun - tain art, Free - ly let me take of thee:
1. Safe in - to the ha - ven guide, O re - ceive my soul at last.
2. Cov - er my de - fence - less head With the sha - dow of thy wing.
3. Spring thou up with - in my heart, Rise to all e - ter - ni - ty.

Words: Charles Wesley (1707-1788)
Music: Charles Wesley and Simeon B. Marsh (1798-1875)

Jesus, Savior, Pilot Me

80

1. Je - sus, Sav - ior, pi - lot me, O - ver life's tem -
2. As a moth - er stills__ her child, Thou canst hush the
3. When at last I near__ the shore, And the fear - ful
1. pes - tuous sea: Un - known waves be - fore me roll, ______
2. o - cean wild; Bois - t'rous waves o - bey thy will ______
3. break - ers roar 'Twixt me and the peace - ful rest ______
1. Hid - ing rocks and treach - 'rous shoal; Chart and com - pass
2. When thou say'st to them, "Be still!" Won - drous Sov - 'reign
3. Then, while lean - ing on thy breast, May I hear thee
1. come _ from thee, Je - sus, Sav - ior, pi - lot me!
2. of ____ the sea, Je - sus, Sav - ior, pi - lot me!
3. say ___ to me, "Fear not- I will pi - lot thee!"

Words: Edward Hopper (1816-1888)
Music: John E. Gould (1822-1875)

Jesus, We Want to Meet

1. Je - sus, we want_ to meet On this_ thy ho - ly day;
2. We kneel in awe_ and fear On this_ thy ho - ly day;
3. Thy bless - ing, Lord,_ we seek On this_ thy ho - ly day;
4. Our minds we ded - i - cate On this_ thy ho - ly day;
1. We gath - er round_ thy throne On this_ thy ho - ly day.
2. Pray God to teach_ us here On this_ thy ho - ly day.
3. Give joy of thy vic - to - ry On this_ thy ho - ly day.
4. Heart and soul con - se - crate On this_ thy ho - ly day.
1. Thou_ art_ our heaven - ly Friend, Hear our prayers as they as - cend;
2. Save_ us_ and cleanse our hearts, Lead and guide our acts of praise,
3. Through grace a - lone are we saved; In thy flock may we be found;
4. Ho - ly Spir - it make us whole; Bless the ser - mon in this place;
1. Look in - to our hearts and minds to - day, On this_ thy ho - ly day.
2. And our faith from seed to flow - er raise, On this_ thy ho - ly day.
3. Let the mind of Christ a - bide in us On this_ thy ho - ly day.
4. And_ as we go,_ lead us Lord; On this_ thy ho - ly day.

Words: A. T. Olajide, 1949; tr. Biodun Adebesin; verses, Austin C. Lovelace, 1962.
Music: Nigerian Folk Song; tr. A. T. Olajide; harm. Carl Haywood (b. 1949), from *Songs of Praise*, Harm. Copyright © 1992. Tr. and Versification Copyright © 1964 Abingdon Press. Reprinted from *The Book of Hymns* by permission.

Just When I Need Him

1. Just when I need Him, Je - sus is near,
2. Just when I need Him, Je - sus is true,
3. Just when I need Him, Je - sus is strong,
4. Just when I need Him, He is my all,
1. Just when I fal - ter, just when I fear; Read - y to help me,
2. Ne - ver for - sak - ing all the way through; Giv - ing for bur - dens
3. Bear - ing my bur - dens all the day long; For all my sor - row
4. An - swer - ing when up - on Him I call; Ten - der - ly watch - ing
1. read - y to cheer, Just when I need Him most.
2. plea - sures a - new, Just when I need Him most.
3. giv - ing a song, Just when I need Him most.
4. lest I should fall, Just when I need Him most.
Just when I need Him most, Just when I need Him most;
Je - sus is near to com - fort and cheer, Just when I need Him most.

Words: William C. Poole (1875-1949)
Music: Charles H. Gabriel (1856-1932)

Just a Little Talk With Jesus

1. I once was lost in sin but Je - sus took me in,
2. Some - times my path seems drear, with - out a ray of cheer,
3. I may have doubts and fears, my eyes be filled with tears,
1. And then a lit - tle light from heav - en filled my soul;
2. And then a cloud of doubt may hide the light of day;
3. But Je - sus is a friend who watch - es day and night;
1. It bathed my heart in love and wrote my name a - bove,
2. The mists of sin may rise and hide the star - ry skies,
3. I go to Him in pray'r, He knows my ev - 'ry care.
1. And just a lit - tle talk with Je - sus made me whole.
2. And just a lit - tle talk with Je - sus clears the way.
3. And just a lit - tle talk with Je - sus makes it right.

Words: Cleavant Derricks
Music: Cleavant Derricks

Have a lit - tle talk with Je - sus,
Now let us let us
tell Him all a - bout our trou - bles, Hear our faint - est cry,
He will and He will
an - swer by and by; Feel a lit - tle pray'r wheel turn - ing,
Now when you and you
know a lit - tle fire is burn - ing,
you will
Find a lit - tle talk with Je - sus makes it right.
it makes it right.

King Jesus Is a-Listenin'

King Je-sus is a-lis-ten-in' all day long, King Je-sus is a-lis-ten-in'
all day long, King Je-sus is a lis-ten-in' all day long, To
hear some sin-ner pray.
Fine
1. That Gos-pel train is com-in', A-rum-blin' through the lan', But I hear them wheels a-hum-min', Get ready to board that train!
2. I know I been con-vert-ed, I ain't gon' make no a-larm, For my soul is bound for glo-ry, And the dev-il can't do me no harm.
3. Some say that John the Bap-tist was noth-in' but a Jew, But the Ho-ly Bi-ble tells us That John was a preach-er too.
D.C.

Words: Traditional
Music: Negro Spiritual; arr. Carl Haywood (b. 1949), from *The Haywood Collection of Negro Spirituals*,

Let All That Is Within Me Cry Holy

Let all that is with - in me __ cry, 1. "Ho - ly!" Let
2. "Bless - ed!"
3. "Wor - thy!"
all that is with - in me __ cry, 1. "Ho - ly!" Ho - ly!
2. "Bless - ed!" Bless - ed!
3. "Wor - thy!" Wor - thy!
1. Ho - ly! Ho - ly is the Lamb that was slain. ____
2. Bless - ed! Bless - ed is the Lamb that was slain. ____
3. Wor - thy! Wor - thy is the Lamb that was slain. ____

Words: Tr. by Melvin Harrel
Music: Anonymous; arr. Charles High

1. If ___ your life in days gone by, Has not been good and true, ___
2. Per-haps your tem-per is to blame, For man-y wrongs you do, ___
3. If in your home the trou-ble is, The course you should pur-sue, ___
4. And if some sin your soul hath bound With cords you can't un-do, ___
5. May-be to you the world is dark, And com-forts far and few, ___
1. In your own way no long-er try, But let Him fix it for you. ___
2. Take it to God in Je-sus' name, And He will fix it for you. ___
3. Go talk with God, your hand in His, And He will fix it for you. ___
4. At Je-sus' feet go lay it down, And He will fix it for you. ___
5. Let Je-sus own and rule your heart, And He will fix it for you. ___
Let Je-sus fix it for you, ___ He knows just what to do; ___
When-ev-er you pray, let Him have His way, And He will fix it for you. ___

Words: Charles A. Tindley (1851-1933)
Music: Charles A. Tindley; arr. Frederick J. Tindley

More Love to Thee, O Christ

87

1. More love to thee, O Christ, More love to thee!
2. Once earth - ly joy I craved, Sought peace and rest;
3. Then shall my ev - ery breath Sing out your praise;
1. Hear thou the prayer I make On bend - ed knee;
2. Now thee a - lone I seek, Give what is best;
3. This be the on - ly song My heart shall raise;
1. This is my ear - nest plea;
2. This all my prayer shall be:
3. This still my prayer shall be:
More love, O Christ, to Thee,
More love to thee, More love to thee!

'ords: Elizabeth P. Prentiss (1818-1878)
ɩusic: William H. Doane (1832-1915)

1. My faith looks up to thee, Thou lamb of Cal - va - ry, Sav - ior di - vine!
2. May thy rich grace im - part Strength to my faint - ing heart, My zeal in - spire;
3. While life's dark maze I tread, And griefs a - round me spread, Be thou my guide;
4. When ends life's tran - sient dream, When death's cold, sul - len stream Shall o'er me roll;
1. Now hear me while I pray, Take all my guilt a - way; O let me from this day Be whol - ly thine.
2. As thou hast died for me, O may my love to thee Pure, warm, and change - less be A liv - ing fire.
3. Bid dark- ness turn to- day, Wipe so - row's tears a - way; Not let me ev - er stray From thee a - side.
4. Blest Sav - ior, then in love, Fear and dis - trust re - move, O bear me safe a- bove, A ran - somed soul.

Words: Ray Palmer (1808-1887)
Music: Lowell Mason (1792-1872)

My Jesus, I Love Thee

1. My Je - sus, I love ___ thee, I know thou art mine,
2. I love thee be - cause ___ thou hast first lov - ed me,
3. I'll love thee in life, ___ I will love thee in death,
4. In man - sions of glo - ry and end - less de - light,
1. For thee all the fol - lies of sin I re - sign;
2. And pur - chased my par - don on Cal - va - ry's tree;
3. And praise thee as long ___ as thou lend - est me breath;
4. I'll ev - er a - dore ___ thee in heav - en so bright;
1. My gra - cious Re - deem - er, my Sav - ior art thou: ___
2. I love thee for wear - ing the thorns ___ on thy brow: ___
3. And say when the death - dew lies cold ___ on my brow, ___
4. I'll sing with the glit - ter - ing crown ___ on my brow, ___
1. If ev - er I loved ___ thee, my Je - sus, 'tis now.
2. If ev - er I loved ___ thee, my Je - sus, 'tis now.
3. "If ev - er I loved ___ thee, my Je - sus, 'tis now."
4. "If ev - er I loved ___ thee, my Je - sus, 'tis now."

Words: William R. Featherstone (1846-1873)
Music: Adoniram J. Gordon (1836-1895)

No, Not One

1. There's not a friend like the low - ly Je - sus,
2. No friend like Him is so high and ho - ly,
3. There's not an hour that He is not near us,
4. Did ev - er saint find this Friend for - sake Him?
5. Was e'er a gift like the Sav - ior giv - en?
1. No, not one! no, not one! None else could heal all our
2. No, not one! no, not one! And yet no friend is so
3. No, not one! no, not one! No night so dark but His
4. No, not one! no, not one! Or sin - ner find that He
5. No, not one! no, not one! Will He re - fuse us a
1. soul's dis - eas - es, No, not one! no, not one!
2. meek and low - ly, No, not one! no, not one!
3. love can cheer us, No, not one! no, not one!
4. would not take him? No, not one! no, not one!
5. home in heav - en? No, not one! no, not one!
Je - sus knows all a - bout our strug - gles, He will guide till the day is done;

Words: Johnson Oatman, Jr. (1856-1922)
Music: George C. Hugg (1848-1907)

There's not a friend like the low - ly Je - sus, No, not one! no not one!
Give Me Jesus
91
1. In the morn - ing when I rise, In the morn - ing when I
2. Dark ___ mid - night was my cry Dark ___ mid - night was my
3. O ___ when I come to die, O ___ when I come to
1. rise, In the morn - ing when I rise, Give me Je - - sus.
2. cry, Dark ___ mid- night was my cry, Give me Je - - sus.
3. die, O ___ when I come to die Give me Je - - sus.
Give me Je - sus, Give me Je - sus, You may
have all this world, Give me Je - sus.

Words: Traditional
Music: Negro Spiritual; arr. Evelyn D. White. Used by Permission.

6
8
1. Noth-ing be-tween my soul and the Sav-ior, Naught of this world's de-
2. Noth-ing be-tween like world - ly plea-sure, Hab - its of life though
3. Noth-ing be-tween like pride_ or sta-tion: Self_ or friends shall
4. Noth-ing be-tween e'en man-y hard tri - als, Though the whole world a -
1. lu - sive dreams; I have re-nounced all sin - ful plea-sure,
2. harm-less they seem, Must not my heart from Him ev - er sev - er,
3. not in - ter - vene; Though it may cost me much trib - u - la - tion,
4. gainst me con - vene; Watch-ing with prayer and much self de - ni - al.
1. Je - sus is mine, There's noth-ing be - tween.
2. He is my all! There's noth-ing be - tween.
3. I am re-solved! There's noth-ing be - tween.
4. Tri-umph at last, with noth-ing be - tween.
Noth-ing be-tween my
soul and the Sav - ior, So that His bless - ed face may be seen;

Words: Charles A. Tindley (1851-1933)
Music: Charles A. Tindley; arr. J. Edward Hoy (b. 1920)

Noth- ing pre-vent- ing the least of His fa- vor: Keep the way clear! Let noth- ing be - tween.
Give Thanks to the Lord
93
Give thanks to the Lord for He is so good, His mer - cy en -
1.
2.3.4.
dures for - ev - er (for - ev - er.) Give dures for - ev - er. (for -
Fine
ev - er.) 1. To Him a - lone who does might - y won - ders,
2. He made the sun to gov - ern the day - time,
D.C.
1. Who by His un - der - stand - ing made the hea - vens.
2. The moon and stars to gov - ern o'er the night - time.

Words: Brenda Barker (b. 1959)
Music: Ken Barker (b. 1955) and Debi Parker Ladd (b. 1961)

1. O holy Savior! friend unseen, Since on thine arm thou bid'st me lean, Help me, throughout life's changing scene, By faith to cling to thee.
2. What though the world deceitful prove, And earthly friends and joys remove? With patient uncomplaining love, Still I would cling to thee.
3. Though faith and hope awhile be tried, I ask not, need not aught beside: How safe, how calm, how satisfied, The souls that cling to thee.

Words: Charlotte Elliot (1789-1871)
Music: Ulysses Elam; arr. R. Nathaniel Dett (1882-1943)

O How I Love Jesus

1. There is a name I love to hear, I love to sing its worth;
2. It tells me of a Sav-ior's love, Who died to set me free;
3. It tells me what my Fa-ther hath In store for ev - 'ry day,
4. It tells of one whose lov-ing heart Can feel my deep - est woe,
1. It sounds like mu - sic in mine ear, The sweet - est name on earth.
2. It tells me of His pre-cious blood, The sin - ner's per-fect plea.
3. And though I tread a dark-some path, Yields sun - shine all the way.
4. Who in each sor - row bears a part, That none can bear be - low.
O how I love Je - sus, O how I love Je - sus,
O how I love Je - sus, Be-cause He first loved me!

Words: Frederick Whitfield (1829-1904)
Music: American Melody

He Is King of Kings

He is King of kings, He is Lord of Lords;
Je - sus Christ, the first and last _ no man works like Him. He is
1.
2.3.4.
no man works like Him.
Fine
1. He built his throne up in the air _
2. I was but young when I be - gun _
no man works like Him;
1. And called the saints from
2. But now my race is
1. ev - 'er where _
2. al - most won _
no man works like Him. He is
D.S.

Words: Traditional
Music: Negro Spiritual; arr. Horace Clarence Boyer (b. 1935)

Ride on, King Jesus

Ride on, King Je - sus, No man can- a hin- der me.
Je - sus ride on no man can- a
1.
Ride on King Je - sus ride on, no man can- a hin- der me.
2.
Fine
hin - der me. 1. King Je - sus rides a milk- white horse, No man works like
2. I know that my re - deem - er lives,
D.C.
Him, 1. De riv - er Jor - d'n He did cross no man works like Him. Oh
2. And of His bless - ing free - ly gives,

Words: Traditional
Music: Negro Spiritual; arr. Hezekiah Brinson, Jr. (b. 1958)

𝄋
1.4. Praise Him! Praise Him!
2. Glo - ry! Glo - ry! In
3. Ooh ___ Ooh ___
1.4. Praise_ Him! Praise_ Him! Je - sus, Bless - ed
2. all ___ things give Him glo - ry. Je - sus, Bless - ed
3. Ooh ___ Ooh ___ Je - sus, Bless - ed
Fine
1.4. Sav - ior, He's wor - thy to be ___ praised. From the
2. Sav - ior, He's wor - thy to be ___ praised. For
3. Sav - ior, He's wor - thy to be ___ praised. From the

Words: Donnie Harper
Music: Donnie Harper

1. ris - ing of the sun un - til the
2. God is our rock, hope of sal -
3. ris - ing of the sun un - til the
1. go - ing down of the same; He's wor - thy, Je - sus is
2. va - tion; A strong de - li - ver -
3. go - ing down of the same; He's wor - thy, Je - sus is
D.S.
1. wor - thy, He's wor - thy to be praised.
2. er, In Him I will al - ways trust.
3. wor - thy, He's wor thy to be praised.

On Christ the Solid Rock

1. My hope is built on noth-ing less Than Je-sus' blood and
2. When dark-ness veils His love-ly face, I rest on His un-
3. His oath, His cov-e-nant and blood, Sup-port me in the
4. When He shall come with trum-pet sound, O may I then in
1. right-eous-ness; I dare not trust the sweet-est frame, But
2. chang-ing grace; In ev-'ry high and storm-y gale, My
3. whelm-ing flood; When all a-round my soul gives way, He
4. Him be found; Dressed in His right-eous-ness a-lone, Fault-
1. whol-ly lean on Je-sus' name.
2. an-chor holds with-in the veil.
3. then is all my hope and stay.
4. less to stand be-fore the throne.
On Christ, the so-lid Rock, I stand, All
oth-er ground is sink-ing sand, All oth-er ground is sink-ing sand.

Words: Edward Mote (1797-1874)
Music: William B. Bradbury (1816-1868)

Somebody's Knockin' at Your Door

Some - bod - y's knock - in' at your door; Some - bod - y's knock - in' at your door;
O ___ sin - ner, why don't you an - swer? Some - bod - y's knock - in' at your
door. ___
1. Knocks like _ Je - sus,
2. Can't you _ hear Him? Some - bod - y's knock - in' at your door;
3. Je - sus _ calls you,
4. Can't you _ trust Him?
1. Knocks like _ Je - sus,
2. Can't you _ hear Him? Some - bod - y's knock - in' at your door;
3. Je - sus _ calls you,
4. Can't you _ trust Him?
O ___
sin - ner, why don't you an - swer? Some - bod - y's knock - in' at your door. ___

Words: Traditional
Music: Negro Spiritual; harm. Richard Proulx (b. 1937)

Softly and Tenderly Jesus Is Calling

1. Soft - ly and ten - der - ly Je - sus is call - ing,
2. Why should we tar - ry when Je - sus is plead - ing,
3. Time is now fleet - ing, the mo - ments are pass - ing,
4. Oh! for the won - der - ful love He has prom - ised,
1. Call - ing for you and for me; See, on the por - tals He's
2. Plead - ing for you and for me? Why should we lin - ger and
3. Pass - ing for you and for me; Shad - ows are gath - er - ing,
4. Prom - ised for you and for me; Though we have sinned, He has
1. wait - ing and watch - ing, Watch - ing for you and for me.
2. heed not His mer - cies, Mer - cies for you and for me?
3. death beds are com - ing, Com - ing for you and for me.
4. mer - cy and par - don, Par - don for you and for me.
Come home, come home,
Come home, come home,

Words: Will L. Thompson (1847-1909)
Music: Will L. Thompson

Ye who are wea - ry, come home! Ear - nest - ly, ten - der - ly,
Je - sus is call - ing, Call - ing, O sin - ner, come home!
O I Love Him
102
Harmony
O I love Him, O I love Him be -
cause He first loved me, first loved me.
1.

Hymn continues on the next page.

Words: Phillip McIntyre (1952-1991)
Music: Phillip McIntyre

2.
Unison
me.
1. My Jesus came to earth from glory, and now I love to tell His
2. He said He's coming back again; Will we be free from all our
1. story of His life and love for me.
2. sins When Christ, our Lord returns?
1. He gave himself a ransom free, Just to save someone like
2. I know He's coming by and by to take us to His home on
1. me.
2. high.
That's why I praise Him each and ev - 'ry day,
I praise Him each and ev - 'ry day.

Steal a-way, steal a-way, steal a-way to Je - sus!
Fine
Steal a-way, steal a-way home, I ain't got long to stay here!
1. My Lord ___ calls me, He calls me by the thun - der;
2. Green trees are bend-ing, Poor sin - ner stands a - trem - bling;
3. Tomb stones are burst-ing, Poor sin - ner stands a - trem - bling;
4. My Lord ___ calls me, He calls me by the light - ning,
D.C.
The trum-pet sounds with-in-a my soul, I ain't got long to stay here.

ords: Traditional
usic: Negro Spiritual; arr. Edward C. Deas

104 The Lord Is My Shepherd

1. The ______ Lord is my Shep- herd, no want shall I know;
2. Through the val - ley and shad - ow my death though I stray,
3. In the midst of af - flic - tion my ta - ble is spread;
4. Let ______ good- ness and mer - cy, my boun - ti - ful God,
1. I feed in green pas - tures, safe - fold - ed I rest; __
2. Since thou art my guard - ian, no e - vil I fear; __
3. With bless - ings un - meas - ured my cup run - neth o'er; __
4. Still fol - low my steps till I meet Thee a - bove; __
1. He lead - eth my soul where the still wa - ters flow, __
2. Thy rod shall de - fend me, thy staff be my stay; __
3. With per - fume and oil thou a nount - est my head;
4. I seek by the path which my an - ces - tors trod, __
1. Re - stores me when wan- d'ring, re - deems when op - pressed;
2. No ______ harm can be - fall, with my com - fort - er near;
3. O ______ what shall I ask of thy prov - i - dence more?
4. Through the land of their so - journ, thy king - dom of love;

Words: James Montgomery (1771-1854)
Music: Thomas Koschat (1845-1914)

1. Re - stores me when wan-d'ring, re - deems when op - pressed.
2. No harm can be - fall, with my com - fort - er near.
3. O what shall I ask of thy prov - i - dence more?
4. Through the land of their so - journ, thy king - dom of love.

I'm So Glad, Jesus Lifted Me

105

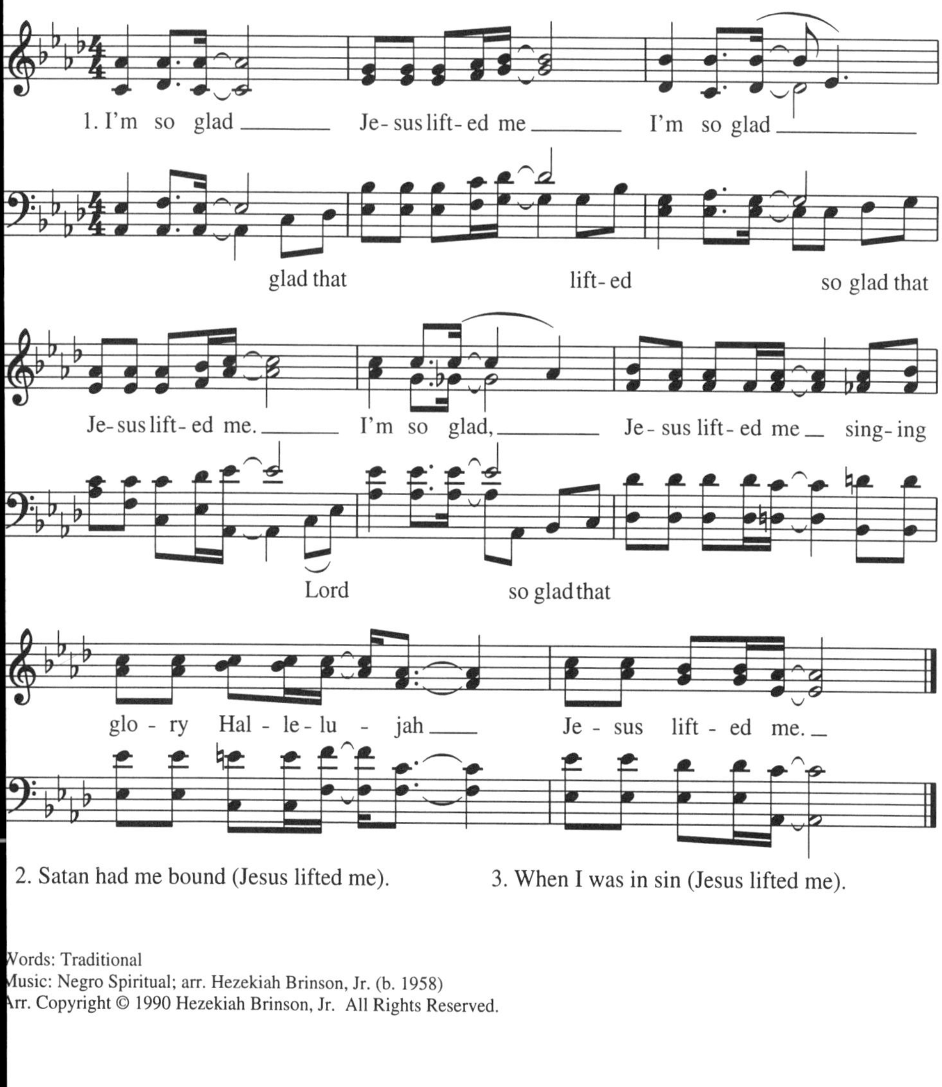

1. I'm so glad Je-sus lift-ed me I'm so glad

glad that lift-ed so glad that

Je-sus lift-ed me. I'm so glad, Je - sus lift-ed me sing-ing

Lord so glad that

glo - ry Hal - le - lu - jah Je - sus lift - ed me.

2. Satan had me bound (Jesus lifted me).

3. When I was in sin (Jesus lifted me).

Words: Traditional
Music: Negro Spiritual; arr. Hezekiah Brinson, Jr. (b. 1958)

Take My Hand, Precious Lord

1. Precious Lord, take my hand, Lead me on, let me stand, I am tired, I am weak, I am worn; Through the storm, through the night, Lead me on to the light, Take my hand, precious Lord, Lead me on.
2. When my way grows drear, precious Lord, linger near, When my life is almost gone; Hear my cry, hear my call, Hold my hand, lest I fall, Take my hand, precious Lord, Lead me on.
3. When the darkness appears and the night draws near, And the day is past and gone; At the river I stand, Guide my feet, hold my hand, Take my hand, precious Lord, Lead me on.

Words: Thomas A. Dorsey (1899–1993)
Music: Thomas A. Dorsey (1899–1993); arr. Horace Clarence Boyer (b. 1935)

There's Something About That Name

Je - sus, Je - sus, Je - sus! There's just some - thing about that name!
Mas - ter, Sav - ior, Je - sus! Like the fra - grance af - ter the rain.
Je - sus, Je - sus, Je - sus! Let all heav - en and earth pro - claim:
Kings and king - doms will all pass a - way, but there's some - thing a - bout that name!

Words: Gloria (b. 1942) and William Gaither (b. 1936)
Music: William J. Gaither

1. 'Tis so sweet to trust in Je - sus, Just to take Him at His word.
2. O how sweet to trust in Je - sus, Just to trust His cleans- ing blood.
3. Yes, 'tis sweet to trust in Je - sus, Just from sin and self to cease.
4. I'm so glad I learned to trust thee, Pre - cious Je - sus, Sa - vior, Friend;
1. Just to rest up - on His prom- ise, Just to know, "Thus saith the Lord."
2. Just in sim - ple faith to plunge me 'Neath the heal - ing, cleans- ing flood!
3. Just from Je - sus sim - ply tak - ing Life and rest and joy and peace.
4. And I know that thou art with me, Wilt be with me to the end.
Je - sus, Je - sus, how I trust Him! How I've proved Him o'er and o'er!
Je - sus, Je - sus, pre - cious Je - sus! O for grace to trust Him more!

Words: Louisa M. R. Stead (1850-1917)
Music: William J. Kirkpatrick (1838-1921)

What a Friend We Have in Jesus

1. What a friend we have in Je - sus, All our sins and griefs to bear!
2. Have we tri - als and temp - ta - tions? Is there trou - ble an - y - where?
3. Are we weak and heav - y lad - en, Cum - bered with a load of care?
1. What a priv - i - ledge to car - ry Ev - 'ry - thing to God in prayer!
2. We should nev - er be dis - cour - aged, Take it to the Lord in prayer.
3. Pre - cious Sav - ior, still our ref - uge, Take it to the Lord in Prayer.
1. Oh, what peace we of - ten for - feit, Oh, what need - less pain we bear,
2. Can we find a friend so faith - ful who will all our sor - rows share?
3. Do thy friends de - spise, for - sake thee? Take it to the Lord in prayer.
1. All be - cause we do not car - ry Ev - 'ry - thing to God in prayer!
2. Je - sus knows our ev - 'ry weak - ness, Take it to the Lord in prayer.
3. In his arms He'll take and shield thee, Thou wilt find a sol - ace there.

ords: Joseph Scriven (1819-1866)
usic: Charles C. Converse (1832-1918)

You Hear the Lambs a-Cryin'

You hear the lambs a-cry-in', hear the lambs a cry-in', hear the lambs a-cry-in' O Shep-herd, feed my sheep. You

1. 2. Fine

feed my sheep.

1. My Sav-ior spoke these words so sweet, say-in'

Oo ___ O Shep-herd, feed my sheep,

"Pe-ter, if you love me, feed my sheep."

D.S.
Oo ___ O Shep-herd, feed my sheep. You

2. O Lord, I love thee, thou dost know;
O Shepherd, feed my sheep.
O give me grace to love thee more.
O Shepherd, feed my sheep.

3. O wasn't that an awful shame?
O Shepherd, feed my sheep.
He hung three hours in mortal pain.
O Shepherd, feed my sheep.

Words: Traditional
Music: Negro Spiritual; harm. Verolga Nix (b. 1933)

Come, Thou Fount of Every Blessing 111

1. Come, Thou fount of every blessing, Tune my heart to sing thy
2. Here I raise my Eb-en-e-zer, Hith-er by thy help I'm
3. O, to grace how great a debt-or, Dai-ly I'm con-strained to

1. grace; Streams of mer-cy nev-er ceas-ing, Call for songs of loud-est
2. come; And I hope, by thy good pleas-ure, Sure-ly to ar-rive at
3. be; Let that grace, Lord, like a fet-ter, Bind my won-d'ring heart to

1. praise. Teach me some me-lo-dious son-net, Sung by flam-ing tongues a
2. home. Je-sus sought me when a stran-ger, Wan-d'ring from the fold of
3. Thee. Prone to wan-der, Lord, I feel_ it, Prone to leave the God I

1. bove. Praise the mount, O fix me on it. Mount of God's un-chang-ing love.
2. God. He, to save my soul from dan-ger, In-ter-posed His pre-cious blood.
3. love. Here's my heart, Lord, take and seal it, Seal it from thy courts a-bove.

ords: Robert Robinson (1735-1790)
usic: *Nettleton*, melody from *A Repository of Sacred Music, Part II*, 1813; harm. Carl Haywood (b. 1949),
om *Songs of Praise*, Harm. Copyright © 1992.

1. Come, Ho - ly Ghost, Cre - a - tor blest, And in our hearts take up thy rest; Come with thy grace and heav'n-ly aid To fill the hearts which thou hast made, To fill the hearts which thou hast made.
2. O Com - fort - er, to thee we cry, Thou heav'n-ly gift of God most high; Thou fount of life, and fire of love, And sweet a - noint - ing from a - bove, And sweet a - nount - ing from a - bove.
3. O Ho - ly Ghost, through thee a - lone, Know we the Fa - ther and the Son; Be this our firm un - chang - ing creed, That thou dost from them both pro - ceed, That thou dost from them both pro - ceed.
4. Praise we the Lord, Fa - ther and Son, And Ho - ly Spir - it with them one; And may the Son on us be - stow All gifts that from the Spir - it flow, All gifts that from the Spir - it flow.

Words: *Veni, Creator Spiritus*; attr. Rabanus Maurus, 776-856; tr. Edward Caswell (1814-1878), alt.
Music: *Lambillotte*, LM; with repeat; Louis Lambillotte, SJ (1796-1855); harm. Richard Proulx (b. 1937)

How Like a Gentle Spirit

1. How like a gen - tle spir - it deep with - in,
2. Let God be God wher - ev - er life may be,
3. God like a moth - er ea - gle hov - ers near,
4. When in our vain pre - ten - sion we con - spire,
1. God reigns our fer - vent pas - sions day by day;
2. let ev - ery tongue bear wit - ness to the call;
3. on might - y wings of pow - er man - i - fest;
4. to shape God's im - age as we see our own;
1. and gives us strength to chal - lenge and to win,
2. all hu - man kind is one by God's de - cree,
3. God like a gen - tle shep - herd stills our fear,
4. hark to the voice a - bove our base de - sire,
1. de - spite the per - ils of our cho - sen way.
2. let God be God let God be God for all.
3. and com - forts us a - gainst a peace - ful breast.
4. God is the sculp - tor, we the bro - ken stone.

5. Through all our fretful claims of sex and race,
the universal love of God shines through;
for God is love transcending style and place,
and all the idle options we pursue.

Words: C. Eric Lincoln (b. 1924). Used by Permission.
Music: Edward John Hopkins (1818-1901)

Ev'ry Time I Feel the Spirit

Harmony
Ev' - ry time I ___ feel the spir - it, ___ mov - ing
in my heart, _ I will pray. ___ Ev' - ry time I ___ feel the
spir - it, ___ mov - ing in my heart, _ I will pray.
Fine
unison
1. Up on the moun - tain my ___ Lord spoke, out of his
2. Jor - dan ri - ver chil - ly and cold, chills ___ the
1. mouth came ___ fire and smoke. ___ All a - round me looked so
2. bod - y but not the soul. ___ There ain't but one train runs this

Words: Traditional
Music: Negro Spiritual

D.C.
1. fine, asked _ my Lord if all was mine. ______
2. track, runs to heav - en and runs right back. ______
Spirit of the Living God
115
Spir - it of the Liv - ing God, Fall fresh on me,
Spir - it of the Liv - ing God, Fall fresh on me.
Melt me, mold me, Fill me, use me.
Spir - it of the Liv - ing God, Fall fresh on me.

/ords: Daniel Iverson (1890-1977)
lusic: Daniel Iverson

Let It Breathe on Me

Let it breathe on me, Let it breathe on me.
Let the breath of the Lord, now, breathe on me,
Let it breathe on me. Let it breathe on me.
Let the breath of the Lord, now, breathe on me.
1. While I'm work - ing Lord in your vine - yard here,
2. When the path - way Lord, I can - not see,
1. I can do naught if thou aren't near.
2. When the way is dark, Lord, breathe on me.

Words: Magnolia Lewis-Butts, 1942
Music: Magnolia Lewis-Butts; harm. W. O. Hoyle

1. Oh, come, bless - ed Lord, just so close to me
2. Give me grace to know when thou art near
1. That I may feel you breathe on me.
2. Oh, I pray thee, Lord, please breathe on me.
'm Goin'-a Sing When the Spirit Says Sing
117
1. I'm goin' - a sing* when the Spir - it says sing.
I'm goin' - a sing when the Spir - it says sing.
I'm goin' - a sing when the Spir - it says sing, and o -
bey the Spi - rit of the Lord.
2. pray 3. moan 4. shout
ords: Traditional
usic: Negro Spiritual; adapt. William Farley Smith (b. 1941)
lapt Copyright © 1989 The United Methodist Publishing House. Reprinted from The United Methodist Hymnal
permission.

1. Oh, let the Son of God en - fold you, with His
2. Oh, come and sing this song with glad - ness, as your
1. Spir - it and His love, Let Him fill your heart and
2. hearts are filled with joy, Lift your hands in sweet sur -
1. sat - is - fy your soul. Oh, let Him
2. ren - der to His name. Oh, give Him
1. have the things that hold you, and His Spir - it like a
2. all your tears and sad - ness, give Him all your years of
1. dove, Will de - scend up - on your life, and make you
2. pain, And you'll en - ter in - to life in Je - sus'

Words: John Wimber
Music: John Wimber

1. whole.
2. name.
Je - sus. Oh,
Je - sus, come and
fill your lambs.
Je - sus, Oh, Je - sus,
come and fill your lambs.

119 Spirit of God, Descend upon My Heart

1. Spir - it of God, de - scend up - on my heart;
2. I ask no dream, no proph - et ec - sta - sies,
3. Teach me to feel that thou art al - ways nigh;
4. Teach me to love thee as thine an - gels love.
1. Draw it from earth; through all its puls - es move;
2. No sud - den rend - ing of the veil of clay,
3. Teach me the strug - gles of the soul to bear,
4. One ho - ly pas - sion fill - ing all my frame;
1. Stoop to my weak - ness, might - y as thou art,
2. No an - gel vis - i - tant, no o - p'ning skies;
3. To check the ris - ing doubt, the reb el sigh;
4. The kin - dling of the heav'n - de - scend - ed dove,
1. And make me love thee as I ought to love.
2. But take the dim - ness of my soul a - way.
3. Teach me the pa - tience of un - an - swered prayer.
4. My heart an al - tar, and thy love the flame.

Words: George Croly (1780-1860)
Music: Frederick C. Atkinson (1841-1897)

1. There's a sweet, sweet Spir - it in this place, And I
(2. There are) bless - ings you can - not re - ceive Till you
(3. If you) say He saved you from your sin, Now you're
1. know that it's the Spir - it of the Lord. There are
2. know Him in His full - ness, and be - lieve. You're the
3. weak, you're bound, and can - not en - ter in, you can

Words: Doris Akers (b. 1922)
Music: Doris Akers

1. sweet ex - pres - sions on each face,
And I
2. one to pro - fit when you say,
"I am
3. make it right if you will yield;
You'll en -
1. know they feel the pres - ence of _ the Lord.
2. going to walk with Je - sus all _ the way."
3. joy the Ho - ly Spir - it that we feel.
Sweet Ho - ly Spir - it, Sweet Heav - en - ly Dove,

Stay right here with us, fill-ing us with your love.
And for these bless-ings we lift our hearts in
praise; With-out a doubt we'll know that we have
been re-vived when we shall leave this place.
1.-2.
3.
2. There are
3. If you place.

121

Baptized in Water

1. Bap-tized in wa-ter, sealed by the Spi-rit, Cleansed by the
2. Bap-tized in wa-ter, sealed by the Spi-rit, Dead in the
3. Bap-tized in wa-ter, sealed by the Spi-rit, Marked with the
1. blood of Christ our King: Heirs of sal-va-tion,
2. tomb with Christ our King: One with his ris-ing.
3. sign of Christ our King: Born of one Fa-ther,
1. trust-ing his prom-ise, Faith-ful-ly now God's praise we sing.
2. freed and for-giv-en, Thank-ful-ly now God's praise we sing.
3. we are his child-ren, Joy-ful-ly now God's praise we sing.

Words: Michael Saward (b. 1932)
Music: Eugene Hancock (b. 1929)

Close to Thee

122

1. Thou my ev - er - last - ing por - tion, More than friend or
2. Not for ease or world - ly pleas - ure, Nor for fame my
3. Lead me through the vale of shad - ows, Bear me o'er life's
1. life to me; All a - long my pil - grim jour - ney,
2. prayer shall be; Glad - ly will I toil and suf - fer,
3. fit - ful sea; Then the gate of life e - ter - nal
1. Sav - ior, let me walk with thee. Close to thee, Close to
2. On - ly let me walk with thee. Close to thee, Close to
3. May I en - ter, Lord, with thee. Close to thee, Close to
1. Thee, Close to thee, Close to thee; All a - long my
2. Thee, Close to thee, Close to thee; Glad - ly will I
3. Thee, Close to thee, Close to thee; Then the gate of
1. pil - grim jour - ney, Sav - ior, let me walk with thee.
2. toil and suf - fer, On - ly let me walk with thee.
3. life e - ter - nal May I en - ter, Lord, with thee.

Words: Fanny J. Crosby (1820-1915)
Music: Silas Vail (1818-1884)

Done Made My Vow

Harmony
Done made my vow to the Lord, And I never will turn back, Oh I will go, I shall go to see what the end will be.
Unison
1. Some-times I'm up, some-times I'm down; See what the end will be, But
2. When I was a mourn-er just like you; See what the end will be, I
Harmony
Unison
1. still my soul is heav'n-ly bound, See what the end will be.
2. prayed and prayed 'til I came through, See what the end will be.
Harmony

Words: Traditional
Music: Negro Spiritual; arr. Evelyn Davidson White. Used by Permission.

Give Me a Clean Heart

Give me a clean heart so I may serve
Thee. Lord, fix my heart so that I may be used by
thee. For I'm not wor - thy of all these bless -

Hymn continues on the next page.

Words: Margaret J. Douroux (b. 1941)
Music: Margaret J. Douroux; harm. Albert Dennis Tessier

ings. Give me a clean heart and I'll fol-low thee
1. I'm not ask-ing for the rich-es of the land.
(2. Some-times) I am up and some-times I am down.
1. I'm not ask-ing for the proud to know my
2. Some-times I am al-most lev-el to the
1. name. Please give me, Lord, a clean heart, that
2. ground. Please give me, Lord, a clean heart, that

1. I may fol - low thee. Give me a clean heart, a
2. I may fol - low thee. Give me a clean heart, a
1. clean heart and I will fol - low thee.
2. Some - times
2. clean heart and I will fol - low thee.
1.
2.

Fix Me, Jesu

Oh, fix me; Oh, fix me;
Je - sus Je - sus
Fine
Oh, fix me; fix me, Je - sus, fix me.
1. Fix me for my long white robe.
2. Fix me for my jour - ney home.
Fix me, Je - sus, fix me.
D.C
1. Fix me for my star - ry crown.
2. Fix me for my dy - ing bed.
Fix me, Je- sus, fix me.

Words: Traditional
Music: Negro Spiritual; arr. Verolga Nix (b. 1933)

Here Am I, Send Me

1. Hark! the voice of Je - sus call - ing, Who will
2. Let none hear you i - dly say - ing, There is
3. Take the task He gives you glad - ly, Let His
1. go and work to - day? Fields are ripe the har - vest
2. noth - ing I can do; While the souls of some are
3. work your pleas - ure be; An - swer quick - ly when He
1. wait - ing, Who will bear the sheaves a - way?
2. dy - ing, And the Mas - ter calls for you.
3. call - eth, "Here am I, send me, send me."
Loud and long the Mas - ter call - eth, Rich re - ward He of - fers free;
Who will an - swer, glad - ly say - ing. "Here am I, send me, send me."

Words: Daniel March
Music: J.C. Lenderman

Oh Lord, I jes' come from de foun - tain, I'm jus' from de foun - tain, Lord, _ I
jes' come from de foun - tain His Name so sweet. Oh Lord, I
1.
2.
Fine
Name so sweet.
1. Po' sin - ner, do you love Je - sus?
2. Class lead - er, do you love Je - sus? Yes, yes, I
3. Zidh' El - der, do you love Je - sus?
do love my Je - sus.
1.Sin - ner, do you love Je - sus?
2.Lead - er, do you love Je - sus? His name so sweet. Oh Lord, I
3.El - der, do you love Je - sus?
D.S.

Words: Traditional
Music: Negro Spiritual; arr. Hall Johnson (1888-1970), from *30 Negro Spirituals for Voice & Piano*

Hush, Hush, Somebody's Callin' My Name

1. Hush, hush, some-bo-dy's cal-lin' my name
1. Hush, Lor-dy, hush, Lor-dy, some-bo-dy's cal-lin' my name. Good Lor-dy,
Hush, hush, some-bo-dy's cal-lin' my name
Hush, Lor-dy, hush, Lor-dy, some-bo-dy's cal-lin' my name
Hush, hush, some-bo-dy's cal-lin' my name Oh my Lord
Hush, Lor-dy, hush, Lor-dy, some-bo-dy's cal-lin' my name. Oh my Lord
Oh my Lord what shall I do? What shall I do?
3
3

2. Sounds like Jesus. Somebody's callin' mah name, ...
3. Soon one mornin', death'll come creepin' in mah room, ...
4. I'm so glad. Ah got my religion in time, ...
5. I'm so glad. I'm on my journey home, ...

Words: Traditional
Music: Negro Spiritual; arr. Moses Hogan. Used by Permission.

I Am Thine, O Lord

1. I am thine, O Lord, I have heard thy voice, And it
2. Con - se - crate me now to thy ser - vice, Lord, By the
3. Oh, the pure de - light of a sin - gle hour That be -
4. There are depths of love that I can - not know Till I
1. told thy love to me; But I long to rise in the
2. pow'r of grace di - vine; Let my soul look up with a
3. fore thy throne I spend, When I kneel in prayer, and with
4. cross the nar - row sea; There are heights of joy that I
1. arms of faith, And be clos - er drawn to thee.
2. stead - fast hope, And my will be lost in thine.
3. thee, my God, I com - mune as friend with friend!
4. may not reach Till I rest in peace with thee.
Draw me near - er, near - er, bless - ed Lord, To the
near - er, near - er,
cross where thou has died, Draw me near - er, near - er,

Words: Fanny J. Crosby (1820-1915)
Music: William H. Doane (1832-1915)

near - er, bless - ed Lord, To thy pre - cious, bleed - ing side.
1. Glo - ry, glo - ry, hal - le - lu - jah!
2. I feel bet - ter, so much bet - ter,
1. Since I laid my bur - den down,
2. Since I laid my bur - den down,
1. Glo - ry, glo - ry, hal - le - lu - jah!
2. I feel bet - ter, so much bet - ter,
1. Since I laid my bur - den down.
2. Since I laid my bur - den down.

lory, Glory, Hallelujah 130

3. Feel like shouting, "Hallelujah!" etc.
4. I am climbing Jacobs ladder. etc.

ords: Traditional
usic: Negro Spiritual; arr. Carl Haywood (b. 1949), from *The Haywood Collection of Negro Spirituals*,

I Know the Lord's Laid His Hands on Me

O I know the Lord, I know the Lord,
I know the Lord's laid His hands on me, O hands on me.
1.
2.
Fine
1. Did ever you see the like before
Jesus preaching to the poor?
2. O wasn't that a happy day
Jesus washed my sins away?
3. Some seek the Lord and don't seek Him right.
fool all day and pray at night.
4. My Lord's done just what He said,
healed the sick and raised the dead.

Words: Traditional
Music: Negro Spiritual; arr R. Nathaniel Dett (1882-1943)

1.
2.
D.C.
1. I know the Lord's _ laid His hands on me, King hands on me.
2. I know the Lord's _ laid His hands on me, When hands on me.
3. I know the Lord's _ laid His hands on me, They hands on me.
4. I know the Lord's _ laid His hands on me, He's hands on me.
132
ert'nly, Lord
1. Have you got good re - li - gion? Cer - t'nly, Lord! _ Have you
got good re - li - gion? Cer - t'nly, Lord! _ Have you
got good re - li - gion? Cer - t'nly, Lord! _
Cer - t'nly, cer - t'nly, cer - t'nly, Lord! _
2. Have you been redeemed? Cert'nly, Lord!
3. Have you been to the water? Cert'nly, Lord!
4. Have you been baptized? Cert'nly, Lord!

ords: Traditional
usic: Negro Spiritual

I Surrender All

1. All to Je - sus I sur - ren - der,
I will ev - er love and trust Him,
2. All to Je - sus I sur - ren - der
World - ly pleas - ures all for - sak - en,
3. All to Je - sus I sur - ren - der
Let me feel the Ho - ly Spir - it
4. All to Je - sus I sur - ren - der
Fill me with thy love and pow - er,
1. All to Him I free - ly give;
In His pres - ence dai - ly live.
2. Hum - bly at His feet I bow;
Take me, Je - sus, take me now.
3. Make me, Sav - ior, whol - ly thine;
Tru - ly know that thou art mine.
4. Lord, I give my - self to thee;
Let thy bless - ings fall on me.
I sur - ren - der all,
I sur - ren - der all,
I su - ren - der all,
I sur - ren - der all.
All to thee, my

Words: Judson W. Van de Vanter (1855-1939)
Music: Winfield S. Weeden (1847-1908)

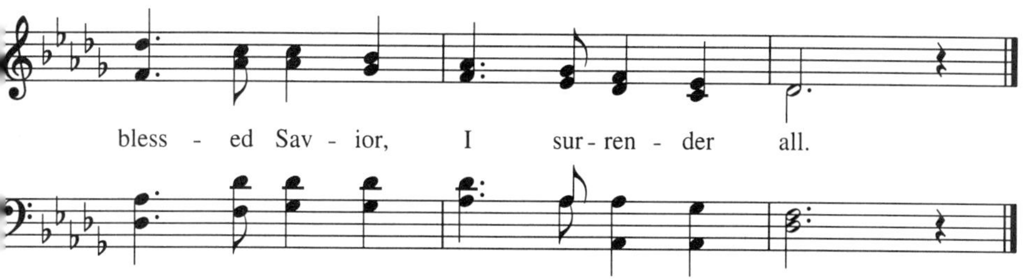
bless - ed Sav - ior, I sur - ren - der all.

Take Me to the Water

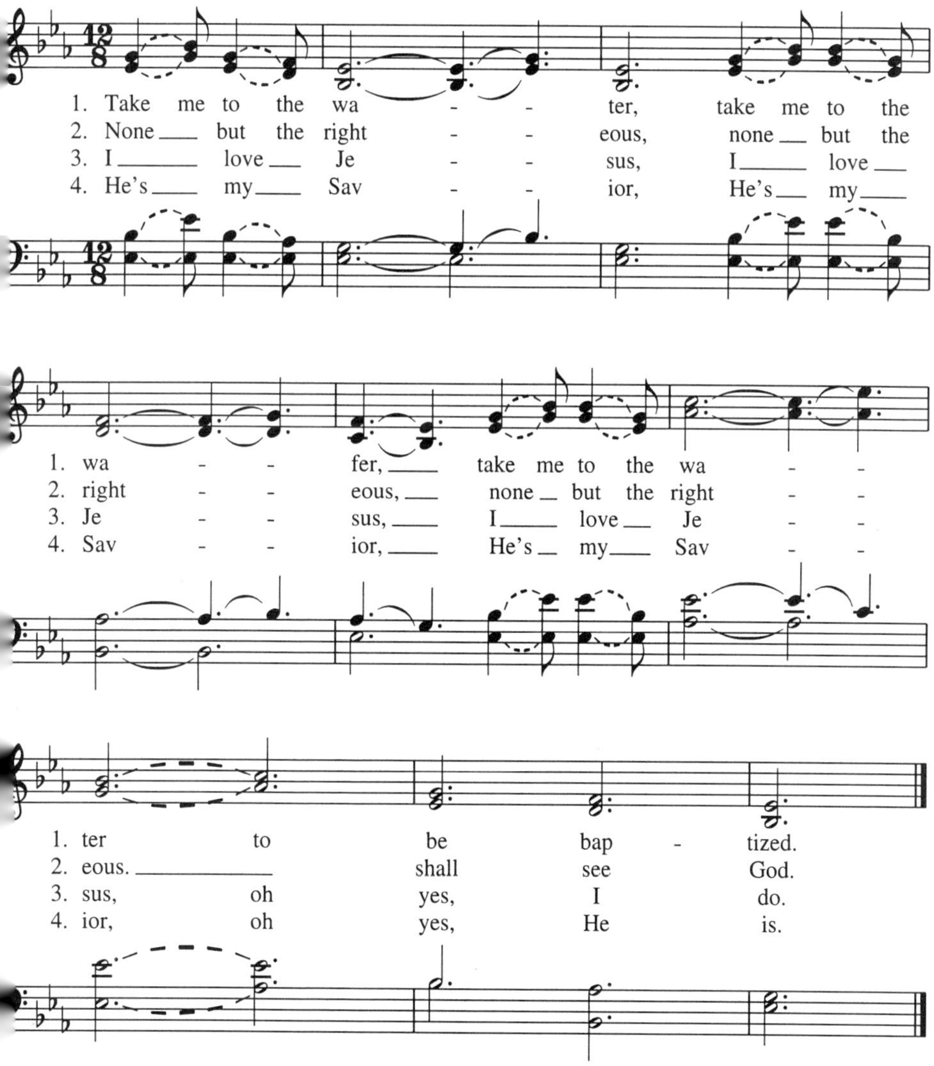

1. Take me to the water, take me to the water, take me to the water to be baptized.
2. None but the righteous, none but the righteous, none but the righteous shall see God.
3. I love Jesus, I love Jesus, I love Jesus, oh yes, I do.
4. He's my Savior, He's my Savior, He's my Savior, oh yes, He is.

rds: Traditional
sic: Negro Spiritual; arr. Horace Clarence Boyer (b. 1935)

Is Your All on the Altar

1. You have longed for sweet peace and for faith to in - crease, And have ear - nest-ly, fer - vent - ly prayed;
2. Would you walk with the Lord in the light of His word, And have peace and con - tent - ment al - way?
3. O we nev - er can know what the Lord will be - stow Of the bless - ings for which we have prayed
4. Who can tell all the love He will send from a - bove, And how hap - py our hearts will be made;
1. But you can - not have rest or be per - fect - ly blest Un - til all on the al - tar is laid.
2. You must do His sweet will to be free from all ill, On the al - tar your all you must lay.
3. Till our bod - y and soul He doth ful - ly con - trol, And our all on the al - tar is laid.
4. Of the char - i - ty sweet we shall share at His feet When our all on the al - tar is laid.

Words: Elisha A. Hoffman (1839-1929)
Music: Elisha A. Hoffman

Is your all on the al - tar of sac - ri - fice laid?
Your heart does the Spir - it con - trol?
You can on - ly be blest and have peace and sweet rest
As you yield Him your bod - y and soul.

1. I have de - cid - ed to fol - low Je - sus,
2. Though no one join me, still I will fol - low,
3. The world be - hind me, the cross be - fore me,
1. I have de - cid - ed to fol - low Je - sus,
2. Though no one join me, still I will fol - low,
3. The world be - hind me, the cross be - fore me,
1. I have de - cid - ed to fol - low Je - sus,
2. Though no one join me, still I will fol - low,
3. The world be - hind me, the cross be - fore me,
No turn - ing back, no turn - ing back!
(no turn - ing back,)

Words: Ascribed to an Indian Prince; as sung in Garo, Assam
Music: Indian Folk Melody; arr. Norman Johnson

Just As I Am

1. Just as I am, without one plea, But
2. Just as I am, though tossed about With
3. Just as I am, poor, wretched, blind; Sight
4. Just as I am, thou wilt receive; Wilt
5. Just as I am, thy love unknown Has
6. Just as I am, of thy great love The
1. that thy blood was shed for me,
2. many a conflict, many a doubt;
3. riches, healing of the mind,
4. welcome, pardon, cleanse, relieve,
5. broken every barrier down;
6. breadth, length, depth, and height to prove,
1. And that thou bidd'st me come to thee, O
2. Fightings and fears within, without, O
3. Yea, all I need in thee to find, O
4. Because thy promise I believe, O
5. Now to be thine, yea, thine alone, O
6. Here for a season, then above: O
Lamb of God, I come, I come. come.

Words: Charlotte Elliott (1789-1871)
Music: William B. Bradbury (1816-1868)

Lord, I Want to Be a Christian

1. Lord, I want to be a Christian In my heart, In my heart; _
2. Lord, I want to be more lov - ing In my heart, In my heart; _
3. Lord, I want to be more ho - ly In my heart, In my heart; _
4. I don't want to be like Ju - das In my heart, In my heart; _
5. Lord, I want to be like Je - sus In my heart, In my heart; _
1. Lord, I want to be a Chris- tian In my heart,
2. Lord, I want to be more lov - ing In my heart,
3. Lord, I want to be more ho - ly In my heart,
4. I don't want to be like Ju - das In my heart,
5. Lord, I want to be like Je - sus In my heart,
In my heart, In my heart,
In my heart, In my heart,
1. Lord, I want to be a Chris- tian In my heart.
2. Lord, I want to be more lov - ing In my heart.
3. Lord, I want to be more ho - ly In my heart.
4. I don't want to be like Ju - das In my heart.
5. Lord, I want to be like Je - sus In my heart.

Words: Traditional
Music: Negro Spiritual; arr. Edward C. Deas

Pass Me Not, O Gentle Savior

139

1. Pass me not, O gen - tle Sav - ior, Hear my hum - ble cry;
2. Let me at thy throne of mer - cy Find a sweet re - lief;
3. Trust - ing on - ly in thy mer - it, Would I seek thy face;
4. Thou the spring of all my com - fort, More than life to me,
1. While on oth - ers thou art call - ing, Do not pass me by.
2. Kneel - ing there in deep con - tri - tion, Help my un - be - lief.
3. Heal my wound - ed, bro - ken spi - rit, Save me by thy grace.
4. Whom have I on earth be - side thee? Whom in heav'n but thee?
Sav - ior, Sav - ior, Hear my hum - ble cry;
While on oth - ers thou art call - ing, Do not pass me by.

Words: Fanny J. Crosby (1820-1915)
Music: William H. Doane (1832-1915)

Lord, I want you to touch me,
Touch me with Thy holy love.
Lord, come down and touch me.
Come down from heaven above.
Lord, reach out and touch me,
Reach out and touch me within,
Lord,

Words: Martha E. Banks
Music: Martha E. Banks; harm. James A. Jones; special harm. Clara Ward (1924-1973)

let good-ness touch me, Thy touch will cleanse me from
Fine
sin.
1. Some folks want trea-sures of sil-ver and
2. Teach me to love and teach me to
1. gold, Some want to reign with pow-ers un-told;
2. pray, Grant me a light to shine day by day;
1. But in my life, all that I can say,
2. Just to a-bide where joys nev-er cease
D.C.
1. Lord, be my guide and have thine own way.
2. Will be great joy, such com-fort and ease.

Shall We Gather at the River

1. Shall we gath-er at the riv-er, Where bright an-gel feet have trod;
2. On the mar-gin of the riv-er, Wash-ing up its sil-ver spray,
3. Ere we reach the shin-ing riv-er, Lay we ev-'ry bur-den down;
4. Soon we'll reach the shin-ing riv-er, Soon our pil-grim-age will cease,
1. With its crys-tal tide for-ev-er Flow-ing by the throne of God?
2. We will walk and wor-ship ev-er, All the hap-py gold-en day.
3. Grace our spir-its will de-liv-er, And pro-vide a robe and crown.
4. Soon our hap-py hearts will quiv-er With the mel-o-dy of peace.
Yes, we'll gath-er at the riv-er, The beau-ti-ful, the beau-ti-ful riv-er;
Gath-er with the saints at the riv-er That flows by the throne of God.

Words: Robert Lowry (1826-1899)
Music: Robert Lowry

Sign me up for the Christian ju - bi - lee,
Sign me up for the Chris- tian ju - bi - lee,
Write my name on heav-en's
Write my name on the roll.
roll. For I've been changed since the Lord has lift - ed
I've been changed since the Lord has lift - ed

Words: Kevin Yancy and Jerome Metcalfe
Music: Kevin Yancy and Jerome Metcalfe; harm. Kenneth Morris (1917-1988)

me, I want to be read - y when Je - sus comes.
me, I want to be read - y when Je - sus comes.
When Je - sus comes, oh, the trum - pet will sound
When Je - sus comes, oh, the trum - pet will sound
loud, Whcn my Sav - ior comes, all the
loud, When my Sav - ior comes, all the

saints in Christ shall rise,
Oh, I'm glad I've been
saints in Christ shall rise,
Ooo,
changed
since He lift - ed me,
Ah,
Ooo,
I
I want to be read - y when Je - sus comes.
want to be read - y when Je - sus comes.

Wade in the Water

Wade in the wa - ter, wade in the wa - ter, chil - dren,
Wade in the wa - ter, God's a-gon-na trou-ble the wa - ter.
Fine
1. See that host all dressed in white,
2. See that band all dressed in red,
3. Look o - ver yon - der, what do I see?
4. If you don't be - lieve I've been re - deemed,
God's a - gon - na trou - ble the wa - ter.
1. The lead - er looks like the Is - ra - elite,
2. Looks like the band that Mo - ses led,
3. The Ho - ly Ghost a - com - ing on me,
4. Just fol - low me down to Jor - dan's stream,
God's a - gon - na trou - ble the wa - ter.
D.C.

Words: Traditional
Music: Negro Spiritual; arr. Carl Haywood (b. 1949), from *The Haywood Collection of Negro Spirituals*, Copyright © 1992.

Where He Leads Me

1. I can hear my Sav - ior call - ing, I can hear my Sav - ior call - ing,
2. I'll go with Him through the gar - den, I'll go with Him through the gar - den,
3. I'll go with Him through the judge- ment, I'll go with Him through the judge- ment,
4. He will give me grace and glo - ry, He will give me grace and glo - ry,
1. I can hear my Sav - ior call - ing, "Take thy cross and fol- low, fol- low me."
2. I'll go with Him through the gar - den, I'll go with Him, with Him, all the way.
3. I'll go with Him through the judge- ment, I'll go with Him, with Him all the way.
4. He will give me grace and glo - ry, And go with me, with me all the way.
Where He leads me I will fol- low, Where He leads me I will fol- low,
Where He leads me I will fol- low, I'll go with Him, with Him all the way.

Words: E. W. Blandy, c. 1890
Music: John S. Norris (1844-1907)

Have Thine Own Way, Lord!

1. Have thine own way, Lord! Have thine own way!
2. Have thine own way, Lord! Have thine own way!
3. Have thine own way, Lord! Have thine own way!
4. Have thine own way, Lord! Have thine own way!

1. Thou art the pot - ter, I am the clay!
2. Search me and try me, Mas - ter, to - day!
3. Wound - ed and wea - ry, Help me, I pray!
4. Hold o'er my be - ing Ab - so - lute sway!

1. Mold me and make me Aft - er thy will,
2. Pur - er than snow, Lord, Wash me just now,
3. Pow er all pow - er Sure - ly is thine!
4. Fill with thy Spir - it 'Til all shall see

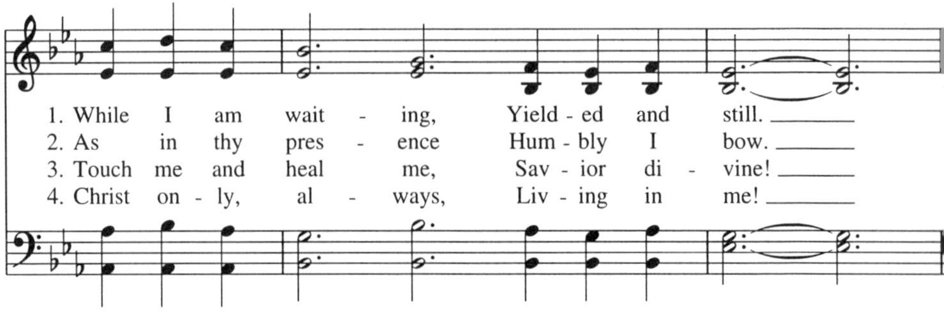
1. While I am wait - ing, Yield - ed and still.
2. As in thy pres - ence Hum - bly I bow.
3. Touch me and heal me, Sav - ior di - vine!
4. Christ on - ly, al - ways, Liv - ing in me!

Words: Adelaide A. Pollard (1862-1934)
Music: George C. Stebbins (1846-1945)

Break Thou the Bread of Life

146

1. Break thou the bread of life, Dear Lord, to me,
2. Bless thou the truth, dear Lord, To me, to me,
3. Teach me to live, dear Lord, On - ly for thee,
1. As thou didst break the loaves Be - side the sea;
2. As thou didst bless the bread By Gal - i - lee;
3. As thy dis - ci - ples lived in Gal - i - lee;
1. Be - yond the sa - cred page I seek thee, Lord;
2. Then shall all bond - age cease, All fet - ters fall,
3. Then, all my strug - gles o'er, Then, vic - t'ry won,
1. My spir - it pants for thee, O liv - ing word!
2. And I shall find my peace, My all in all.
3. I shall be - hold thee, Lord, The liv - ing one.

Words: Mary A. Lathbury (1841-1913)
Music: William F. Sherwin (1826-1888)

1. Come, ye dis - con - so - late, wher - e'er ye lan - guish,
2. Joy of the des - o - late, light ___ of the stray - ing,
3. Here see the bread of life; see ___ wa - ters flow - ing
1. Come to the mer - cy - seat, fer - vent - ly kneel:
2. Hope of the pen - i - tent, fade - less and pure!
3. Forth from the throne of God, pure from a - bove:
1. Here bring your wound - ed hearts, here tell ___ your ___ an - guish;
2. Here speaks the com - fort - er, ten - der - ly ___ say - ing,
3. Come to the feast of love; come, ev - er ___ know - ing
1. Earth ___ has no sor - row that heav'n can - not heal.
2. "Earth ___ has no sor - row that heav'n can - not cure."
3. Earth ___ has no sor - row but heav'n can re - move.

Words: Stanzas 1-2, Thomas Moore (1779-1852); Stanza 3, Thomas Hasting (1784-1872)
Music: Sammuel Webbe (1740-1816)

’m a-Going to Eat at the Welcome Table

148

1. I’m a-going to eat at the wel-come ta - ble,
2. I’m a-going to feast on milk and hon - ey,
3. I’m a-going to fly all a-round in heav - en,
4. I’m a-going to wade cross Jor - dan’s riv - er,
1. I’m a-going to eat at the wel-come ta - ble, some of these days.
2. I’m a-going to feast on milk and hon - ey, some of these days.
3. I’m a-going to fly all a-round in heav - en, some of these days.
4. I’m a-going to wade cross Jor - dan’s riv - er, some of these days.
1. I’m a-going to eat at the wel-come ta - ble, I’m going to
2. I’m a-going to feast on milk and hon - ey, I’m going to
3. I’m a-going to fly all a-round in heav - en, I’m going to
4. I’m a-going to wade cross Jor - dan’s riv - er, I’m going to
1. eat at the wel - come ta - ble, some of these days.
2. feast on milk and hon - ey, some of these days.
3. fly all a-round in heav - en, some of these days.
4. wade ’cross Jor - dan’s riv - er, some of these days.

Words: Traditional
Music: Negro Spiritual; arr. Carl Diton (1886-1969), from *36 South Carolina Spirituals*

In Remembrance of Me

1. In re - mem - brance of me,
2. (In re -) mem - brance of me,
1. eat this bread. In re - mem - brance of me, drink this wine. In re -
2. heal the sick. In re - mem - brance of me, feed the poor. In re -
1. mem - brance of me, pray for the time when God's own will is
2. mem - brance of me, o - pen the door and let your broth - er
1.
2.
done. In re -
in, Let him in.
Take, eat, and be com - fort - ed; drink and re - mem - ber

Words: Ragan Courtney
Music: Buryl Red; arr. Robert F. Douglas

too. That this in my bod - y and pre - cious blood shed for
you, shed for you. In re - mem - brance of me
search for truth. In re - mem - brance of me al - ways love. In re -
mem - brance of me, don't look a - bove, but in your heart
look for God. Do this in re- mem- brance of me

Jesus, the Bread of Life

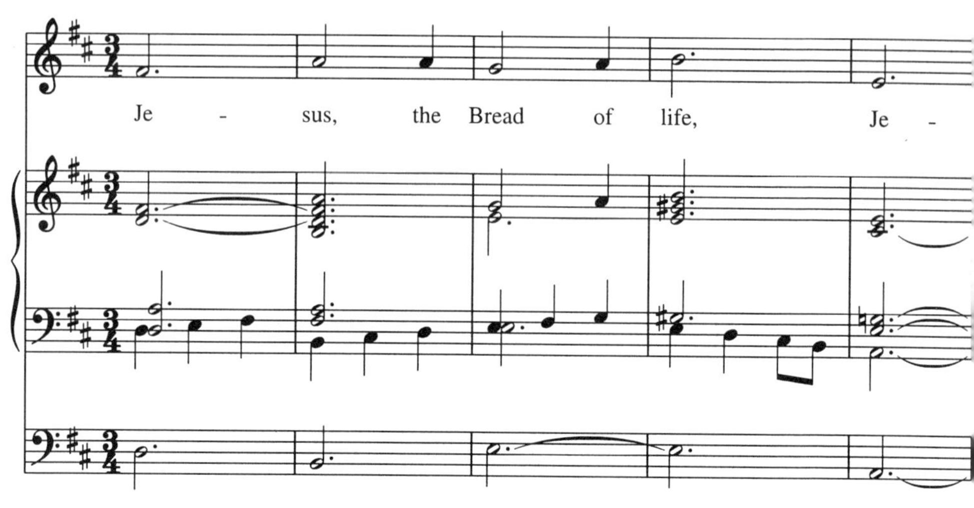
Je - sus, the Bread of life, Je -

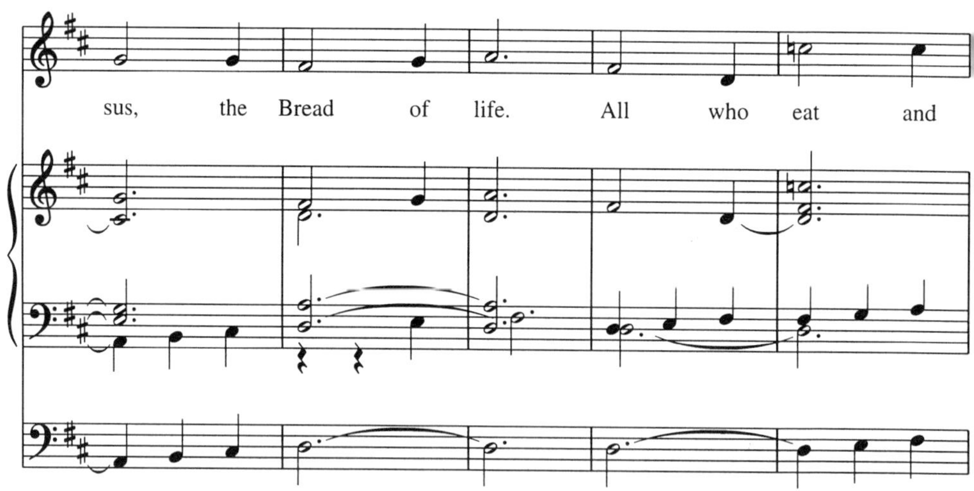
sus, the Bread of life. All who eat and

Words: John 6; Grayson Warren Brown (b. 1948)
Music: Grayson Warren Brown; harm. Michael B. Lynch

drink of Him will nev - er die,
Fine
will nev - er die.
Fine
1. I am the Bread that came down from heav - en.
2. All who come to me will not hun - ger,
3. All who love and keep my com - mand - ments

1. I will be your food.
2. nor will they ev - er thirst.
3. will be loved by my Fa - ther.
1. All who put their trust in me will
2. If you turn to me in faith I'll
3. And we shall both com - fort them and
D.C.
1. nev - er die.
2. nev - er turn a - way.
3. make our home in them.
D.C.

One bread, one bod - y,
one Lord of all,
one cup of
bless - ing which we bless.
And we, though

Words: 1 Corinthians 10:16, 17; 12:4; Galatians 3:28; The Didache 9
Music: John B. Foley, SJ

man - y, through - out the earth, we are one
Last time
bod - y in this one Lord.
Last time
1. Gen - tile or Jew, ser - vant or
2. Man - y the gifts, man - y the
3. Grain for the fields, scat - tered and

1. free, wom - an or man,
2. works, one in the Lord
3. grown, gath - ered to one
D.S.
1. no more. One
2. of all. One
3. for all. One
D.S.
CODA
Lord.

1. Let us break bread to - geth - er on our knees (on our
2. Let us drink wine to - geth - er on our knees (on our
1. knees); Let us break bread to - geth- er on our knees (on our
2. knees); Let us drink wine to - geth- er on our knees (on our
1. knees).
2. knees).
When I fall on my knees, with my face to the ris - ing
sun, Oh ___ Lord, have mer - cy on me (on me). me).
1.
2.

Words: Traditional
Music: Negro Spiritual; arr. Carl Haywood (b. 1949), from *The Haywood Collection of Negro Spirituals*,

Let us praise God to-geth-er on our knees (yes, on our knees); Let us
praise God to-geth-er on our knees (yes on our knees). When I
fall on my knees, with my face to the ris-ing sun, Oh ___
Lord, have mer-cy on me (on me).

Lord I Have Seen Thy Salvation

1. Lord I have seen thy sal - va - tion, Lord I have seen thy sal
2. Lord I have heard of thy king - dom, Lord I have heard of thy
1. va - tion, drank of the blood, held the
2. pro - mise, looked on thy birth, cried at
1. bo - dy, Lord I have seen, seen with my eyes, seen with my
2. Cal - v'ry, Lord I have heard, Lord I have heard, Lord I have

Words: John D. Cooper (b. 1925)
Music: John D. Cooper

1. heart.
2. heard.
Fell on my knees, down at the al - tar, bowed down my
head, whisp - ered a pray - er.
Have mer - cy
Lord, I'm not wor - thy, I be -
lieve, Yes, I be - lieve, now I am sure.

Taste and see. Taste and see the good - nes

of the Lord. O Taste and see. Taste and

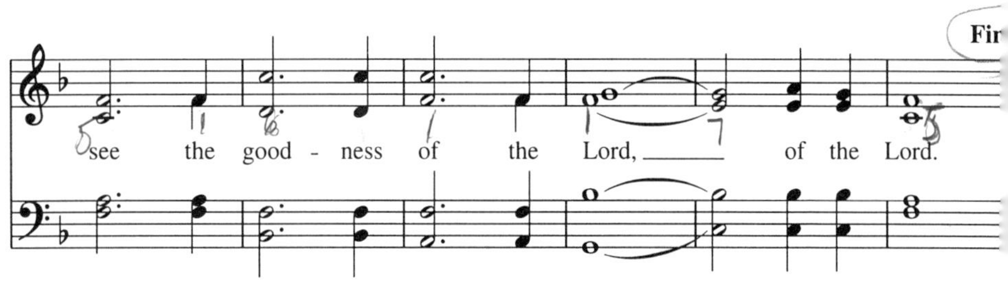
see the good - ness of the Lord, of the Lord.
Fi

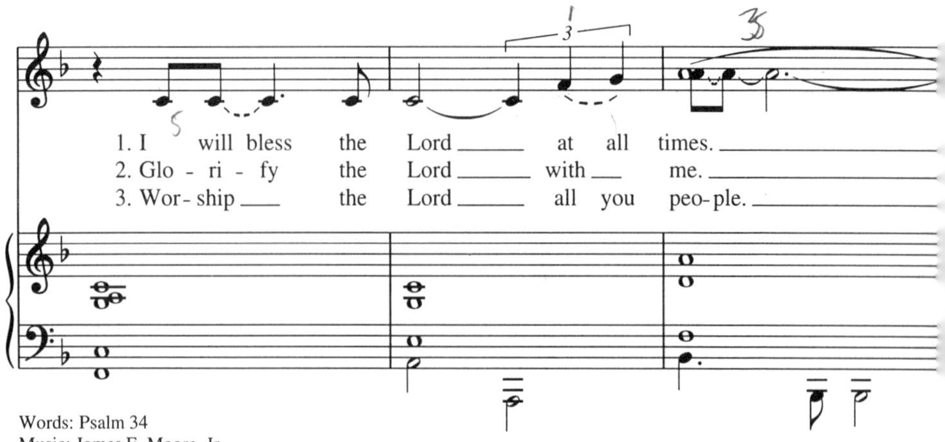
1. I will bless the Lord at all times.
2. Glo - ri - fy the Lord with me.
3. Wor- ship the Lord all you peo- ple.
3

Words: Psalm 34
Music: James E. Moore, Jr.

1. His praise shall al - ways be on my
2. To - geth - er let us all praise His
3. You'll want for noth - ing if you
1. lips; my soul shall
2. name. I called the
3. ask. Taste and
1. glo - ry in the Lord; for
2. Lord and He ans - swered me; from
3. see that God is good; in
D.C.
1. He has been so good to me.
2. all my trou - bles He set me free.
3. Him we need put all our trust.

This Is My Bod

This is my bod - y ___ giv-en up for you, ___ this is my

blood ___ poured out for you. ___ This is my bod - y ___ giv - en

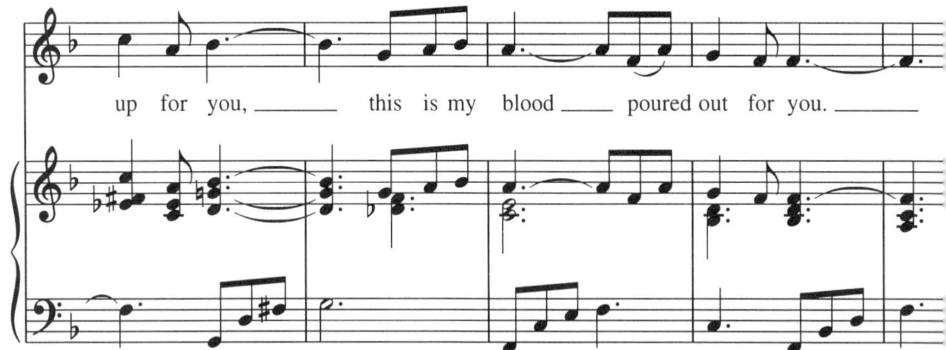
up for you, ___ this is my blood ___ poured out for you. ___

Words: From *Mary, Cause of Our Joy*
Music: Edward V. Bonnemere

Bod-y of Christ, A - men, Blood of
Christ, A - men, Bod-y of Christ.
A - men, Blood of Christ, A - men.

156

Come to Me

1. "Come to me, Ye who are hard _ op - pressed;
2. "Come to me!" Je - ho - vah gen - tly pleads;
1. Lay your head gen - tly up - on _ my breast; _
2. "Come to me, I can sup - ply _ all needs; _
1. Come to me, And I will give _ you rest; wea - ry
2. And my way, Un - to green pas - ture leads; Free from
1. one, Hith - er come! God is your home!"
2. sin! En - ter in! God is your home!"

Words: Traditional
Music: Negro Spiritual; arr. R. Nathaniel Dett (1882-1943)

1. We praise thee, O God, For the son of thy
2. We praise thee, O God, For thy spir - it of
3. All glo - ry and praise To the lamb that was
4. Re - vive us a - gain, Fill each heart with thy
1. love, For Je - sus who died And is now gone a - bove.
2. light, Who has shown us our Sav - ior, And scat - tered our night.
3. slain, Who has borne all our sins And has cleansed ev - 'ry stain.
4. love, May each soul be re - kin - dled With fire from a - bove.
Hal - le - lu - jah! Thine the glo - ry, Hal - le - lu - jah! A -
men, Hal - le - lu - jah! Thine the glo - ry, Re - vive us a - gain.

Words: William P. MacKay (1837-1885)
Music: John H. Husband (1760-1825)

1. Out in the high - ways and by - ways of life,
2. Tell the sweet sto - ry of Christ and His love,
3. Give as 'twas giv - en to you in your need,
1. Man - y are wea - ry and sad;
2. Tell of His power to for - give;
3. Love as the Mas - ter loved you;
1. Car - ry the sun - shine where dark - ness is rife,
2. Oth - ers will trust Him if on - ly you prove
3. Be to the help - less a help - er in - deed,
1. Mak - ing the sor - row - ing glad.
2. True, ev - ery mo - ment you live.
3. Un - to your mis - sion be true.

Words: Ira B. Wilson (1880-1950)
Music: George Schuler (1882-1973)

Make me a bless - ing, Make me a bless - ing,
Out of my life May Je - sus shine;
Make me a bless - ing, O Sav - ior, I pray,
Make me a bless - ing to some - one to - day.

1. How to reach the mass - es, those of ev - 'ry birth, For an
2. Oh! the world is hun - gry for the liv - ing bread, Lift the
3. Don't ex - alt the preach - er, don't ex - alt the pew, Preach the
4. Lift Him up by liv - ing as a chris - tian ought, Let the
1. an - swer Je - sus gave the key; "And I, if I be lift - ed
2. Sav - ior up for them to see; Trust Him and do not doubt the
3. gos - pel sim - ple, full and free; Prove Him and you will find that
4. world in you the Sav - ior see; Then all will glad - ly fol - low
1. up from the earth, Will draw all men* un - to Me."
2. words that He said, "I'll draw all men* un - to Me."
3. prom - ise is true, "I'll draw all men* un - to Me."
4. Him who once taught, "I'll draw all men* un - to Me."
Lift Him up, Lift Him up,
Lift the pre - cious sav - ior up, Lift the pre - cious sav - ior up,
Still He speaks from e - ter - ni - ty: "And I, if I be lift - ed

Words: Johnson Oatman, Jr. (1856-1922)
Music: B. B. Beall

up from the earth, Will draw all men* un - to Me."

*"folk" may be substituted for "men."

This Little Light of Mine 160

1. This lit - tle light of mine, ___ I'm goin' - a let it shine, ___
this lit - tle light of mine, ___ I'm goin' - a let it shine, ___
this lit - tle light of mine, ___ I'm goin' - a let it shine,
let it shine, let it shine, let it shine (let it shine).

2. Everywhere I go...
3. All through the night...

Words: Traditional
Music: Negro Spiritual; adapt. William Farley Smith (b. 1941)

1. "Go preach my gos - pel," saith the Lord, "Bid the whole earth my grace re - ceive, Ex - plain to them my sa - cred word, Bid them be - lieve, o - bey, and live."
2. "I'll make my great com - mis - sion known, And ye shall prove my gos - pel true By all the works that I have done, And all the won - ders ye shall do."
3. "Go heal the sick, go raise the dead, Go cast out dev - ils in my name. Nor let my proph - ets be a - fraid, Though man re - proach, and will blas - pheme."
4. "While thus ye fol - low my com - mands, I'm with you till the world shall end. All pow'r in trust - ed in my hands; I can de - stroy, and can de - fend."
5. He spake and light shone round His head, On a bright cloud to heav'n He rode. They to the far - thest na - tion spread The grace of their as - cend - ed God.

Words: Isaac Watts (1674-1748)
Music: Thomas Hastings (1784-1872)

ome by Here *(Kum bah-ya)*

1. Come by here Lord, come by here,
Come by here Lord, come by here,
Come by here Lord, come by here,
O Lord, come by here.

Someone needs you Lord, come by here.

3. Send a blessing Lord, come by here.

ords: Traditional
usic: Negro Spiritual; arr. Richard Smallwood
r. used by permission of Century Oak/Richwood Music.

Come Here Jesus, If You Pleas

No harm have I done you on my knees, (on my knees,) No
harm have I done you on my knees, (on my knees,) When you see me
on my knees, dear Lord, come here, Jesus, if you
please.
A - men,
A - men, A -
men, A - - - men.

Words: Roland M. Carter (b. 1942)
Music: Roland M. Carter

Do Lord, Remember Me

1. Do Lord, do Lord, Do re-mem-ber me,
2. When I'm in trou-ble, Do re-mem-ber me,
3. When I'm dy-in', Do re-mem-ber me,
4. When this world's on fire, Do re-mem-ber me,
1. Do Lord, do Lord, Do re-mem-ber me,
2. When I'm in trou-ble, Do re-mem-ber me,
3. When I'm dy-in', Do re-mem-ber me,
4. When this world's on fire, Do re-mem-ber me,
1. Do Lord, do Lord, Do re-mem-ber me,
2. When I'm in trou-ble, Do re-mem-ber me,
3. When I'm dy-in', Do re-mem-ber me,
4. When this world's on fire, Do re-mem-ber me,
O
Do Lord re-mem-ber me.

Words: Traditional
Music: Negro Spiritual; arr. John W. Work (1901-1967). Used by permission of Mrs. J. W. Work.

Higher Ground

1. I'm press - ing on the up - ward way, New heights I'm
2. My heart has no de - sire to stay Where doubts a -
3. I want to live a - bove the world, Though sa - tan's
4. I want to scale the ut - most height, And catch a
1. gain - ing ev - ery day; Still pray - ing as I on - ward bound,
2. rise and fears dis - may; Though some may dwell where these a - bound,
3. darts at me are hurled; For faith has caught a joy - ful sound,
4. gleam of glo - ry bright; But still I'll pray till heav'n I've found,
1. "Lord, plant my feet on high - er ground."
2. My prayer, my aim is high - er ground.
3. The song of saints on high - er ground.
4. "Lord, lead me on to high - er ground."
Lord, lift me
up, and let me stand By faith, on heav - en's ta - ble - land; A high - er
plane than I have found, Lord, plant my feet on high - er ground.

Words: Johnson Oatman, Jr. (1860-1948)
Music: Charles H. Gabriel (1856-1932)

Lord, my soul is thirst - ing for a bless - ing to - day,
Let thy pre - sence come from a - bove;
O that thou wouldst rend the heav - ens;
and then come down;
Let thy spir - it fall all a - round.
Lord, my soul is thirst - ing and I want a re - fresh - ing;
Lord, my soul is thirst - ing and I need a fresh touch.
Lord, my soul is thirst - ing and I want a re - fresh - ing.
Grant me a bless - ing to - day.

Hymn continues on the next page.

Words: Joseph N. Heard
Music: Joseph N. Heard

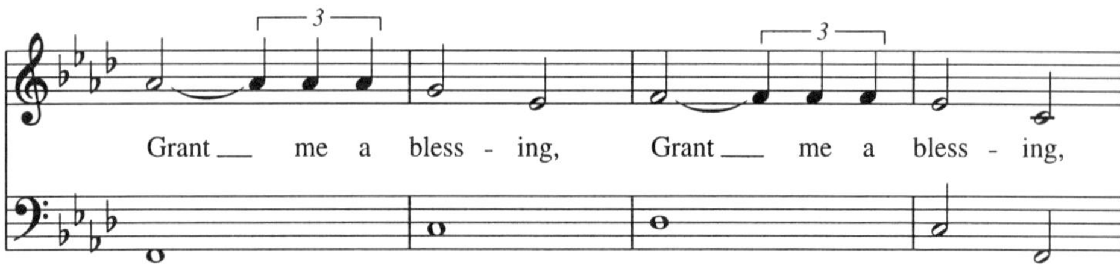
Grant __ me a bless - ing, Grant __ me a bless - ing,

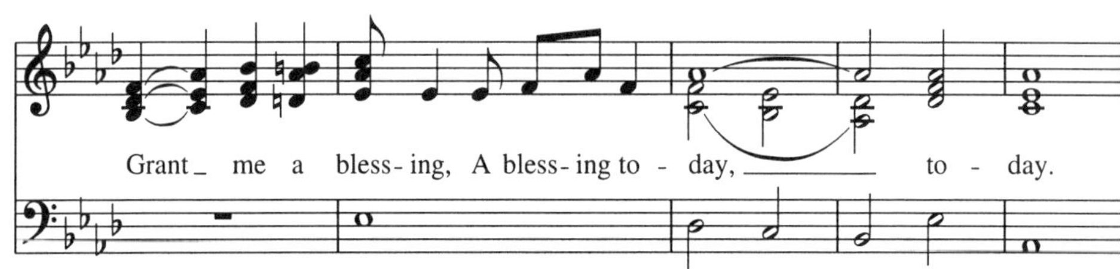
Grant _ me a bless-ing, A bless-ing to - day, ________ to - day.

167 Even M

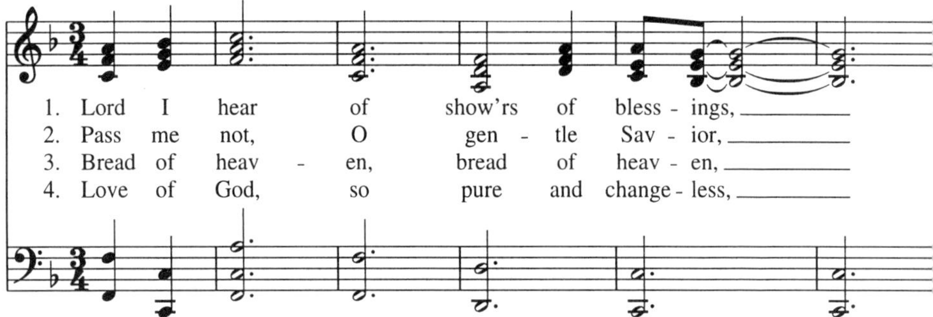
1. Lord I hear of show'rs of bless - ings, ________
2. Pass me not, O gen - tle Sav - ior, ________
3. Bread of heav - en, bread of heav - en, ________
4. Love of God, so pure and change - less, ________

1. Thou are scat - t'ring full and free; ________
2. Sin - ful though my heart may be; ________
3. Ev - er let me feed on thee; ________
4. Blood of Christ, so rich, so free; ________

Words: Traditional
Music: Negro Spiritual; harm. Roberta Martin (1912-1969)

1. Show'rs the thirst - y souls re - fresh - ing,
2. I am long - ing for thy fa - vor,
3. Vine of heav - en, vine of heav - en,
4. Grace of God, so strong and bound - less,
1. Let some drops now fall on me!
2. Whilst thou'rt bless - ing, Oh bless me!
3. Let thy blood a - tone for me!
4. Mag - ni - fy them all in me!
E - ven me, yes! E - ven me!
E - ven me, Lord! E - ven me!
1. Let some drops now fall on me!
2. Whilst thou'rt bless - ing, Lord, bless me!
3. Let thy blood a - tone for me!
4. Mag - ni - fy them all in me!

I Am Praying for You

1. I have a Sav - ior, He's plead - ing in glo - ry,
2. I have a Fa - ther, to me He has giv - en
3. I have a robe: 'tis re - splen - dent in white - ness,
4. When Je - sus has found you, tell oth - ers the sto - ry,
1. A dear, lov - ing sav - ior, though earth - friends be few;
2. A hope for e - ter - ni - ty, bless - ed and true;
3. A - wait - ing in glo - ry my won - der - ing view;
4. That my lov - ing sav - ior is your sav - ior, too;
1. And now He is watch - ing in ten - der - ness o'er me,
2. And soon will He call me to meet Him in heav - en,
3. Oh, when I re - ceive it all shin - ing in bright - ness,
4. Then pray that your Sav - ior may bring them to glo - ry,
1. And, oh, that my Sav - ior were your sav - ior, too.
2. But, oh, that He'd let me bring you with me, too!
3. Dear friend, could I see you re - ceiv - ing one, too!
4. And prayer will be an - swered, 'twas an - swered for you!

Words: S. O'Malley Cluff
Music: Ira D. Sankey (1840-1908)

For you I am pray - ing, For you I am pray - ing,
For you I am pray - ing, I'm pray - ing for you.
Sometimes I Feel Like a Motherless Chile
169
1. Some - times I feel like a moth - er - less chile,
2. Some - times I feel like I'm al - mos' gone,
1. Some - times I feel like a moth - er - less chile,
2. Some - times I feel like I'm al - mos' gone,
1. Some - times I feel lika a moth - er - less chile,
2. Some - times I feel like I'm al - mos' gone,
A

Hymn continues on the next page.

Words: Traditional
Music: Negro Spiritual; arr. Carl Haywood (b. 1949), from *The Haywood Collection of Negro Spirituals*,

long ways from home, A long

ways from home. Then I get down on my knees an'

pray, Get down on my knees an' pray.

170

Yield Not to Temptation

1. Yield not to temp - ta - tion, For yield - ing is sin;
2. Shun e - vil com - pan - ions, Bad lan - guage dis - dain;
3. To him that o'er - com - eth, God giv - eth a crown;

Words: Horatio R. Palmer (1834-1907)
Music: Horatio R. Palmer; arr. Carl Haywood (b. 1949), from *Songs of Praise*, Harm. Copyright © 1992.

1. Each vic-t'ry will help you, Some o-ther to win;
2. God's name hold in rev - 'rence, Nor take it in vain;
3. Through faith we will con - quer, Though oft - en cast down;
1. Fight, still pres-sing on - ward, Dark pas-sions sub - due;
2. Be thought-ful and ear - nest, Kind - heart - ed and true;
3. He who is our sav - ior, Our strength will re - new;
Look ev - er to Je - sus, He will car - ry you through.
Ask the sav - ior to help you, Com - fort, strength - en and keep you;
He is will - ing to aid you, He will car - ry you through.

I Couldn't Hear Nobody Pray

O ___ Lord ___
O, I could-n't hear no-bod-y pray, could-n't hear no-bod-y
O Lord, I

pray. O, way down yon-der by ___ my-self, And I

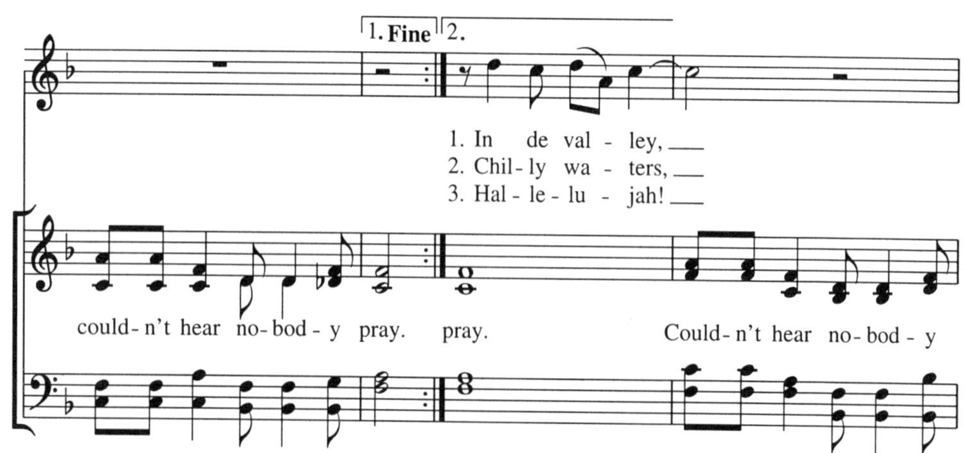
1. Fine
2.
1. In de val-ley, ___
2. Chil-ly wa-ters, ___
3. Hal-le-lu-jah! ___
could-n't hear no-bod-y pray. pray. Could-n't hear no-bod-y

Words: Traditional
Music: Negro Spiritual; arr. Carl Haywood (b. 1949), from *The Haywood Collection of Negro Spirituals*,

1. On ma knees,
2. In de Jer-den,
3. Trou-bles o - ver
Wid ma bur-den,
Cross-in' o - ver,
In de king-dom,
pray, Could-n't hear no-bod-y pray, Could-n't hear no-bod-y
D.S.
1. An' ma Sav - ior.
2. In - to Ca - naan.
3. Wid my Je - sus.
O ma Lord,
D.S.
pray, Could-n't hear no-bod - y pray, I

Nobody Knows the Trouble I See, Lor

No - bod - y knows the trou - ble I see, Lord,
No - bod - y knows the trou - ble I see;
No - bod - y knows the
trou - ble I see, Lord,
No - bod - y knows but Je - sus.
Fin
Broth - er, will you pray for me? Broth - er, will you pray for me?
Broth - er, will you pray for me, And help me to drive old sa - tan a - way?
D.C

Words: Traditional
Music: Negro Spiritual; arr. R. Nathaniel Dett (1882-1943)

2. Sister, will you pray for me?
Sister, will you pray for me?
Sister, will you pray for me,
And help me to drive old satan away?

3. Father, will you pray for me?
Father, will you pray for me?
Father, will you pray for me,
And help me to drive old satan away?

4. Mother, will you pray for me?
Mother, will you pray for me?
Mother, will you pray for me,
And help me to drive old satan away?

Keep Me Every Day

173

1. Lord, I want to live _ for thee, Ev - 'ry day _ and hour;
2. In my weak-ness be _ my strength; In my tri - als all,
3. Leave me not to walk _ a - lone, Lest I droop _ and die;
1. Let thy spi - rit be _ with me, In its sav - ing pow'r!
2. Be thou near me all _ the day, Hear my ev - 'ry call!
3. Let thy spir - it go _ with me, And at - tend _ my cry!
Keep my heart, and keep my hand, Keep my soul, I pray!
Keep my tongue to speak _ thy praise, Keep me all _ the way!

Words: F. L. Eiland
Music: Emmet S. Dean

Let the Heav'n Light Shine on Me

Let the heav'n light shine on me, Let the heav'n light shine on
me, for ___ low is the way to the up - per bright world, Let the
heav'n light shine on me. Shine on me, Shine on
me. ___ Let the light ___ from heav'n ___ shine ___ on
A - men, A - men.
me. A - men, A - men.

Words: Roland M. Carter (b. 1942)
Music: Roland M. Carter

Nobody Knows the Trouble I've Seen

No - bod - y knows the trou - ble I've seen,
No - bod - y knows but Je - sus,
No - bod - y knows the trou - ble I've seen,
Glo - ry, hal - le - lu - jah.
Fine
1. Some - times I'm up, some - times I'm down, Oh, yes, Lord, Some -
2. Al - though you see me going 'long so, Oh, yes, Lord, I
1. times I'm al - most to the ground, Oh, yes, Lord.
2. have my trou - bles here be - low, Oh, yes, Lord.
D.C.

Words: Traditional
Music: Negro Spiritual

1.2.3.
D.C.
4.
1. If I have wound - ed an - y soul to - day,
2. If I have ut - tered i - dle words or vain,
3. If I have been per - verse, or hard, or cold,
4. For - give the sins I have con - fessed to thee;
1. If I have caused one foot to go a - stray,
2. If I have turned a - side from want or pain,
3. If I have longed for shel - ter in the fold,
4. For - give the se - cret sins I do not see;
1. If I have walked in my own will - ful way,
2. Lest I of - fend some oth - er through the strain,
3. When thou hast giv - en me some fort to hold,
4. O guide me, love me, and my keep - er be.
Dear Lord, for - give (for - give)!
A - men (A - men).

Words: C. M. Battersby
Music: Charles Gabriel (1856-1932)

Standin' in the Need of Prayer 177

It's me, it's me, O Lord, Stand - in' in the need of prayer;
It's me,
It's me, It's me, O Lord, Stand - in' in the need of prayer.
It's me,
Fine
1. Not my broth - er, not my sis - ter, but it's me, O Lord,
2. Not the preach - er, not the dea - con, but it's me, O Lord,
3. Not my fa - ther, not my moth - er, but its me, O Lord,
4. Not the stran - ger, not my neigh - bor, but it's me, O Lord,
1. Stand - in' in the need of prayer, Not my broth - er, not my sis - ter, but it's
2. Stand - in' in the need of prayer, Not the preach - er, not the dea - con, but it's
3. Stand - in' in the need of prayer, Not my fa - ther, not my moth - er, but its
4. Stand - in' in the need of prayer, Not the stran - ger, not my neigh - bor, but it's
D.C.
1. me, O Lord, Stand - in' in the need of prayer.
2. me, O Lord, Stand - in' in the need of prayer.
3. me, O Lord, Stand - in' in the need of prayer.
4. me, O Lord, Stand - in' in the need of prayer.

Words: Traditional
Music: Negro Spiritual; arr. Carl Haywood (b. 1949), from *The Haywood Collection of Negro Spirituals*,

1. Sweet hour of prayer, sweet hour of prayer, That calls me from a
2. Sweet hour of prayer, sweet hour of prayer, Thy wings shall my pe
3. Sweet hour of prayer, sweet hour of prayer, May I thy con - so
1. world of care, And bids me at my Fa - ther's throne Make
2. ti - tion bear To Him whose truth and faith - ful - ness En -
3. la - tion share, Till from Mount Pis - gah's loft - y height I
1. all my wants and wish - es known. In sea - sons of dis -
2. gage the wait - ing soul to bless; And since He bids me
3. view my home and take my flight: This robe of flesh I'll
1. tress and grief My soul has of - ten found re - lief.
2. seek His face, Be - lieve His word and trust His grace.
3. drop, and rise To seize the ev - er - last - ing prize.

Words: William Walford (1772-1850)
Music: William B. Bradbury (1816-1868)

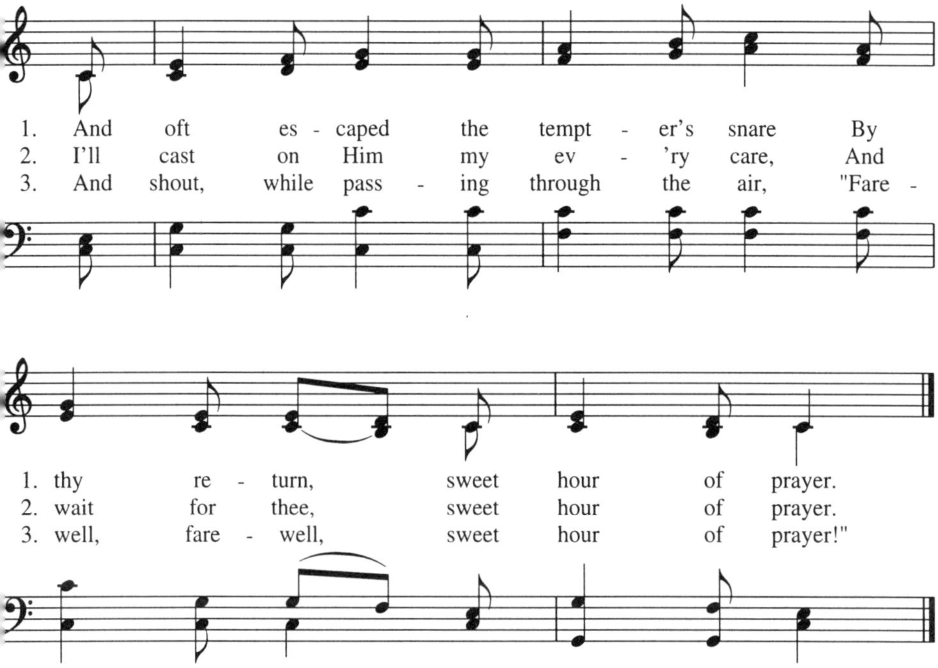

1. And oft es - caped the tempt - er's snare By
2. I'll cast on Him my ev - 'ry care, And
3. And shout, while pass - ing through the air, "Fare -

1. thy re - turn, sweet hour of prayer.
2. wait for thee, sweet hour of prayer.
3. well, fare - well, sweet hour of prayer!"

Remember Me 179

Re - mem - ber me, Re - mem - ber
me, O Lord, re - mem - ber me.

Words: Traditional
Music: Negro Spiritual; harm. J. Jefferson Cleveland (1937-1988)

180 **Ain'-a That Good News**

I got a
1. I got a robe up in - a that king-dom ain'-a that good news, Ain'-a that good news.
robe up in - a that king - dom ain'- a that good news.
Ain'- a that good news. I'm a gon-na
lay down this world gon - na should - er up - a my cross. Gon - na
take it home - a to my Je - sus ain'- a that good news, (ain'- a that good news.)

2. I got a crown up in-a that kingdom.

3. I got a savior in-a that kingdom.

Words: Traditional
Music: Negro Spiritual; arr. Clayton White (b. 1942)

Amazing Grace

181

1. A - maz - ing grace! how sweet the sound, That
2. 'Twas grace that taught my heart to fear, And
3. The Lord has prom - ised good to me, His
4. Through man - y dan - gers, toils, and snares, I
5. When we've been there ten thou - sand years, Bright
1. saved a wretch like me! I once was lost, but
2. grace my fears re - lieved; How pre - cious did that
3. word my hope se - cures; He will my shield and
4. have al - read - y come; 'Tis grace that brought me
5. shin - ing as the sun, We've no less days to
1. now am found, Was blind, but now I see.
2. grace ap - pear The hour I first be - lieved!
3. por - tion be As long as life en - dures.
4. safe thus far, And grace will lead me home.
5. sing God's praise Than when we'd first be - gun.

Words: Stanzas 1-4, John Newton, (1725-1807); Stanza 5, Ascr. John Rees, c. 1859
Music: *New Britain*, CM, *Virginia Harmony*, 1831; harm. John Barnard (b. 1948)

Didn't My Lord Deliver Daniel

Refrain
Did - n't my Lord de - liv - er Dan - iel, ___ de - liv - er
Dan - iel, ___ de- liv - er Dan - iel, ___ Did - n't my Lord de - liv - er
Dan - iel, ___ An' ___ why not a ev - e - ry man. ___
Fine
Verse 1.
He de - liv - ered Dan - iel from the li - on's den, an'
Jo-nah from the bel - ly of the whale; An' the He - brew chil - dren from the
fie - ry fur - nace, An' why not ev - e - ry man.
D.C. Refrain

Words: Traditional
Music: Negro Spiritual; arr. Carl Haywood (b. 1949), from *The Haywood Collection of Negro Spirituals*,

Verse 2.
The win' blows eas' an' de win' blows wes', It
blows like de judg-a-ment __ day; An' ev-ry po' soul __ dat
D.C. Refrain
nev-er did pray 'll be glad to pray __ dat day.
Verse 3.
I set my foot on de gos-pel ship, an' de
ship be-gin __ to __ sail; It land-ed me o-ver on
D.C. al Fine
Ca-naan's shore, _ An' I'll nev-er come back __ no more.

1. Be not dis - mayed what - e'er be - tide, God will take care of you;
2. Through days of toil when heart doth fail, God will take care of you;
3. All you may need He will pro - vide, God will take care of you;
4. No mat - ter what may be the test, God will take care of you;
1. Be - neath His wings of love a - bide, God will take care of you.
2. When dan - gers fierce you path as - sail, God will take care of you.
3. Noth - ing you ask will be de - nied, God will take care of you.
4. Lean, wea - ry one, up - on His breast, God will take care of you.
God will take care of you, Through ev - 'ry day, O'er all the way;
He will take care of you, God will take care of you.

Words: Civilla D. Martin (1869-1948)
Music: W. Stillman Martin (1862-1935)

Blessed Assurance 184

1. Bless-ed as - sur - ance, Je - sus is mine! O what a
2. Per - fect sub - mis - sion, per-fect de - light, Vi - sions of
3. Per - fect sub - mis - sion, all is at rest, I in my
1. fore-taste of glo - ry di-vine! Heir of sal - va - tion, pur-chase of
2. rap - ture now burst on my sight; An - gels de-scend - ing, bring from a -
3. sav - ior am hap - py and blest; Watch-ing and wait - ing, look-ing a -
1. God, Born of His spir - it, washed in His blood.
2. bove Ech - oes of mer - cy, whis-pers of love.
3. bove, Filled with His good - ness, lost in His love.
This is my sto - ry, this is my song, Prais-ing my

Hymn continues on the next page.

Words: Fanny J. Crosby (1820-1915)
Music: Phoebe P. Knapp (1839-1908)

sav - ior all the day long; ___ This is my sto - ry, this is my
song, ___ Prais - ing my sav - ior all the day long. ___

185 Blessed Quietnes

1. Joys are flow - ing ___ like a riv - er,
2. Bring - ing life and ___ health and glad - ness
3. Like the rain that ___ falls from heav - en,
4. See, a fruit - ful ___ field is grow - ing,
5. What a won - der - ful sal - va - tion,

1. Since the com - fort - er has come; ___
2. All a - round this heav'n - ly guest, ___
3. Like the sun - light from the sky, ___
4. Bless - ed fruit of righ - teous ness; ___
5. When we al - ways see His face, ___

Words: Marie P. Ferguson
Music: W. S. Marshall; arr. J. Jefferson Cleveland (1937-1988) and Verolga Nix (b. 1933)

1. He a - bides with us for - ev - er,
2. Ban - ished un - be - lief and sad - ness,
3. So the Ho - ly Ghost is giv - en,
4. And the streams of life are flow - ing
5. What a per - fect hab - i - ta - tion,
1. Makes the trust - ing heart His home.
2. Chang'd our wea - ri - ness to rest.
3. Com - ing on us from on high.
4. In the lone - ly wil - der - ness.
5. What a qui - et rest - ing place.
Bless-ed qui-et-ness, ho - ly qui-et-ness, What as-sur-ance in my soul,
On the storm-y sea, Je-sus speaks to me, And the bil-lows cease to roll.

I Can Do All Things Through Christ

I can do all things through Christ who strength - ens me.
I can do all things through Christ who strength- ens me.
I can do all things through Christ, I can do all things through Christ, I can do all things through Christ who strength - ens me, strength - ens me.

Words: Eibernita Clark
Music: Eibernita Clark

Farther Along

1. Tempt - ed and tried we're oft made to won - der, Why it should
2. When death has come and tak - en our loved ones, It leaves our
3. Faith - ful till death said our lov - ing mas - ter, A few more
4. When we see Je - sus com-ing in glo - ry, When He comes
1. be thus all the day long; While there are oth - ers liv-ing a -
2. home so lone-ly and drear; Then do we won - der why oth - ers
3. days to la-bor and wait; Toils of the road will then seem as
4. from His home in the sky; Then we shall meet Him in that bright
1. bout us, Nev-er mo - lest - ed though in the wrong.
2. pros - per, Liv-ing so wick - ed year af - ter year.
3. noth - ing, As we sweep through the beau-ti - ful gate.
4. man - sion, We'll un - der - stand it all by and by.
Far - ther a - long we'll know all a - bout it, Far-ther a -

Hymn continues on the next page.

Words: W. B. Stevens
Music: W. B. Stevens; arr. J. R. Baxter, Jr.

long we'll un-der-stand why; Cheerup, don't wor - ry, live in the
sun - shine, We'll un - der - stand it all by and by.

188 It Is Well with My Soul

1. When peace, like a riv - er, at - tend - eth my
2. Though sa - tan should buf - fet, though tri - als should
3. My sin— oh, the bliss of this glo - ri - ous
4. And, Lord, haste the day when the faith shall be

1. way, When sor - rows like sea - bil - lows roll;
2. come, Let this blest as - sur - ance con - trol,
3. thought— My sin— not in part, but the whole—
4. sight, The clouds be rolled back as a scroll,

Words: Horatio Spafford (1828-1888)
Music: Philip P. Bliss (1838-1876)

1. Whatever my lot, thou hast taught me to
2. That Christ has regarded my helpless es-
3. Is nailed to the cross and I bear it no
4. The trump shall resound and the Lord shall de-
1. say, It is well, it is well with my soul.
2. tate, And has shed His own blood for my soul.
3. more, Praise the Lord, praise the Lord, O my soul!
4. scend, "Even so"— it is well with my soul.
It is well with my soul,
It is well with my soul,
It is well, it is well with my soul.

189 Great Is Thy Faithfulness

1. Great is thy faith - ful-ness, O God my Fa - ther,
2. Sum - mer and win - ter, and spring-time and har - vest,
3. Par - don for sin and a peace that en - dur - eth,
1. There is no shad - ow of turn - ing with thee;
2. Sun, moon and stars in their cours - es a - bove,
3. Thine own dear pres - ence to cheer and to guide;
1. Thou chang - est not, thy com - pas - sions, they fail not,
2. Join with all na - ture in man - i - fold wit - ness,
3. Strength for to - day and bright hope for to - mor - row,
1. As thou hast been thou for - ev - er wilt be.
2. To thy great faith - ful-ness, mer - cy and love.
3. Bless - ings all mine, with ten thou - sand be - side!

Words: Thomas O. Chisholm (1866-1960)
Music: William M. Runyan (1870-1957)

Great is thy faith - ful - ness! Great is thy faith - ful - ness!
Morn - ing by morn - ing new mer - cies I see;
All I have need - ed thy hand hath pro - vid - ed,
Great is Thy faith - ful - ness, Lord un - to me!

He'll Understand, and Say "Well Done

1. If ___ when you give ___ the best ___ of your ser - vice, ___
2. Mis - un - der - stood, ___ the sav - ior of sin - ners, ___
3. If ___ when this life ___ of la - bor is end - ed, ___
4. But ___ if you try ___ and fail ___ in your try - ing, ___
1. Tell - ing the world ___ that the Sav - - ior has come; ___
2. Hung ___ on the cross; ___ He was God's ___ on - ly Son; ___
3. And ___ the re - ward ___ of the race ___ you have run; ___
4. Hands ___ sore and scarred ___ from the work ___ you've be - gun; ___
1. Be ___ not dis - mayed ___ when friends ___ won't be - lieve you; ___
2. Oh! ___ hear him call ___ His fa - ther in heav - en, ___
3. Oh! ___ the sweet rest ___ pre - pared ___ for the faith - ful, ___
4. Take ___ up your cross, ___ run quick - ly to meet Him, ___
1. He'll ___ un - der - stand, ___ and say ___ "well done." ___
2. "Not ___ my will, ___ but thine ___ be done." ___
3. Will ___ be His blest ___ and fi - nal ___ "well done." ___
4. He'll ___ un - der - stand, ___ and say, ___ "well done." ___

Words: Lucie E. Campbell (1885–1963)
Music: Lucie E. Campbell (1885–1963); arr. Horace Clarence Boyer (b. 1935)

Oh, when I come to the end of my Journey,
wea - ry of life, and the bat - tle is won.
Car - r'ing the staff and the cross of re-demp-tion
He'll un-der - stand, and say "Well done".

191

His Eye Is on the Sparrow

1. Why should I feel dis - cour - aged, ___ Why should the shad - ows come, ___
2. "Let not your heart be trou - bled," _ His ten - der word I hear, ___
3. When ev - er I am tempt - ed, ___ When ev - er clouds a - rise, ___
1. Why should my heart be lone - ly, ___ And long for heav'n and home; ___ Whe
2. And rest - ing on His good - ness, _ I lose my doubts and fears; ___ Thou
3. When songs give place to sigh - ing, _ When hope with - in me dies, ___ I
1. Je - sus is ___ my por - tion? ___ My con - stant friend _ is He: ___ His
2. by the path _ He lead - eth, ___ But one step I ___ may see; ___ His
3. draw the clos - er to Him, ___ From care He sets _ me free; ___ His
eye is on ___ the spar - row, _ And I know He watch - es me; ___ His

Words: Civilla D. Martin (1860-1948)
Music: Charles H. Gabriel (1856-1932); arr. Horace Clarence Boyer (b. 1935)

eye is on the spar - row, and I know He watch-es me. I
sing be - cause I'm hap - py, I sing be - cause I'm free; For His
eye is on the spar - row, And I know He watch - es me.

I Need Thee Every Hou

1. I need thee ev - 'ry hour, Most gra - cious
2. I need thee ev - 'ry hour, Stay thou near
3. I need thee ev - 'ry hour, In joy or
4. I need thee ev - 'ry hour, Teach me thy

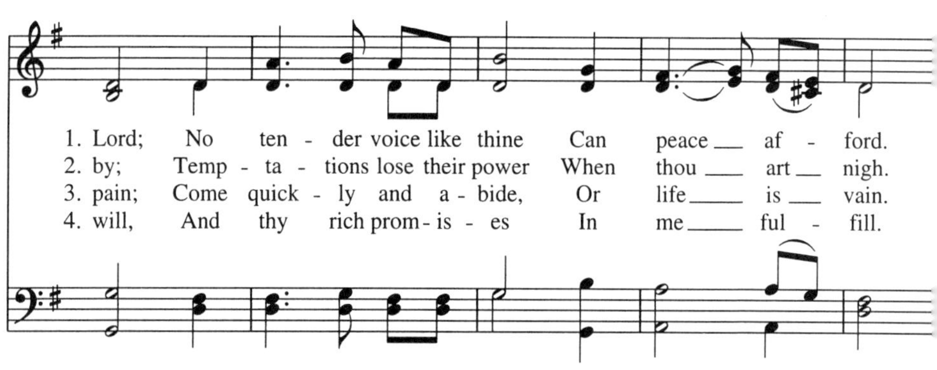
1. Lord; No ten - der voice like thine Can peace af - ford.
2. by; Temp - ta - tions lose their power When thou art nigh.
3. pain; Come quick - ly and a - bide, Or life is vain.
4. will, And thy rich prom - is - es In me ful - fill.

I need thee, O I need thee, Ev - 'ry hour I need thee; O

bless me now, my sav - ior, I come to thee.

Words: Annie S. Hawks (1835-1918)
Music: Robert Lowry (1826-1899)

I Will Trust in the Lord

1. I will trust in the Lord, I will trust in the
2. Sis-ter will you trust in the Lord, Sis-ter will trust in the
1. Lord, I will trust in the Lord 'til I die;
2. Lord, Sis-ter will you trust in the Lord 'til you die;
1. I will trust in the Lord, I will trust in the
2. Sis-ter will you trust in the Lord, Sis-ter will you trust in the
1. Lord, I will trust in the Lord 'til I die.
2. Lord, Sis-ter will you trust in the Lord 'til you die.

3. Brother will you trust in the Lord ('til you die).
4. I'm gonna treat my neighbor right ('til I die).
5. I'm gonna hold my savior's hand ('til I die).

Words: Traditional
Music: Negro Spiritual; arr. Carl Haywood (b. 1949), from *The Haywood Collection of Negro Spirituals*,

Lead Me, Guide Me

Lead _ me, guide _ me, a - long the way,
For ___ if you lead me, I can - not stray.
Lord, ___ let me walk each day with Thee.
Lead me, Oh Lord, lead me. ___
Fine

Words: Doris M. Akers (b. 1922)
Music: Doris M. Akers; arr. Richard Smallwood

1. I am weak and I need thy strength and power to
2. Help me tread in the paths of right - eous - ness, be my
3. I am lost if you take your hand from me, I am
1. help me o - ver my weak - est hour; Help me
2. aid when sa - tan and sin op - press; I am
3. blind with - out thy light to see; Lord, just
1. through the dark - ness thy face to see,
2. put - ting all my trust in thee.
3. al - ways let me thy ser - vant be.
D.C.
1. Lead me, Oh Lord, lead me.
2. Lead me, Oh Lord, lead me.
3. Lead me, Oh Lord, lead me.

1. I've been 'buked an' I've been scorned,
2. Dere is trou-ble all o-ver dis worl',
3. Ain' gwine lay my 'li-gion down,
1. I've been 'buked an' I've been scorned, chil-dren;
2. Dere is trou-ble all o-ver dis worl', chil-dren;
3. Ain' gwine lay my 'li-gion down, chil-dren;
1. I've been 'buked an' I've been scourned,
2. Dere is trou-ble all o-ver dis worl',
3. Ain' gwine lay my 'li-gion down,
1. I've been talked a-bout sho's you' born.
2. Dere is trou-ble all o-ver dis worl'.
3. Ain' gwine lay my 'li-gion down.

Words: Traditional
Music: Negro Spiritual; arr. Carl Haywood (b. 1949), from *The Haywood Collection of Negro Spirituals*, Copyright © 1992.

Leaning on the Everlasting Arms

1. What a fel - low-ship, what a joy di - vine,
2. O how sweet to walk in this pil - grim way,
3. What have I to dread, what have I to fear,
1. Lean - ing on the ev - er - last - ing arms; What a bless - ed - ness,
2. Lean - ing on the ev - er - last - ing arms; O how bright the path
3. Lean - ing on the ev - er - last - ing arms; I have bless - ed peace
1. what a peace is mine, Lean - ing on the ev - er - last - ing arms.
2. grows from day to day, Lean - ing on the ev - er - last - ing arms.
3. with my Lord so near, Lean - ing on the ev - er - last - ing arms.
Lean - ing, lean - ing, safe and se-curefrom all a-larms;
Lean-ing on Je-sus, lean - ingon Je-sus,
Lean - ing, lean - ing, Lean-ing on the ev - er - last- ing arms.
Lean-ingon Je - sus, lean-ingon Je - sus

Words: Elisha A. Hoffman (1839-1929)
Music: Anthony J. Showalter (1858-1924); arr. Carl Haywood (b. 1949), from *Songs of Praise*, Copyright © 1992.

Leave It There

1. If the world from you with - hold, of its sil - ver and its gold,
2. If your bod - y suf - fers pain, and your health you can't re - gain,
3. When your en - e - mies as - sail, and your heart be - gins to fail,
4. When your youth - ful days are gone, and old age is steal - ing on.
1. And you have to get a - long with mea - ger fare;
2. And your soul is al - most sink - ing in de - spair;
3. Don't for - get that God in heav - en an - swers prayer;
4. And your bod - y bends be - neath the weight of care;
1. Just re - mem - ber in His word. How He feeds the lit - tle bird.
2. Je - sus knows the pain you feel. He can save and He can heal.
3. He will make a way for you, and will lead you safe - ly through.
4. He will nev - er leave you then, He'll go with you to the end.
1. Take your bur - den to the Lord and leave it there.
2. Take your bur - den to the Lord and leave it there.
3. Take your bur - den to the Lord and leave it there.
4. Take your bur - den to the Lord and leave it there.
(leave it there)

Words: Charles A. Tindley (1851-1933)
Music: Charles A. Tindley; arr. Verolga Nix (b. 1933)

Leave it there, leave it there,
Leave it there, leave it there, leave it there, leave it there,
leave it there.
Take your bur - den to the Lord and leave it there, leave it there.
If you trust and nev - er doubt, He will sure - ly bring you out;
leave it there.
Take your bur - den to the Lord and leave it there, leave it there.

Love Lifted Me

1. I was sink - ing deep in sin, Far from the peace - ful shore,
2. All my heart to Him I give, Ev - er to Him I'll cling,
3. Souls in dan - ger, look a - bove, Je - sus com - plete - ly saves;
1. Ver - y deep - ly stained with - in, Sink - ing to rise no more;
2. In His bless - ed pres - ence live, Ev - er His praise - es sing.
3. He will lift you by His love Out of the an - gry waves.
1. But the mas - ter of the sea Heard my de - spair - ing cry,
2. Love so might - y and so true Mer - its my soul's best songs;
3. He's the mas - ter of the sea, Bil - lows His will o - bey;
1. From the wa - ters lift - ed me— Now safe am I.
2. Faith - ful, lov - ing ser - vice, too, To Him be - longs.
3. He your sav - ior wants to be— Be saved to - day.
Love lift - ed me, Love lift - ed me,
Love lift - ed e - ven me, Love lift - ed e - ven me, When noth - ing

Words: James Rowe (1865-1933)
Music: Howard E. Smith (1863-1918)

1.
2.
else could help, Love lift - ed me; Love lift-ed me.
Don't Feel No Ways Tired
199
I don't feel no ways tired, I come too
far from where I start - ed from; No-bod - y
told me that the road would be eas - y, I
don't be - lieve He brought me this far to leave me.

Words: Curtis Burrell
Music: Curtis Burrell; harm. Kenneth Morris (1917-1988)

1. When the storms of life are rag - ing,
2. In the midst of trib - u - a - tions,
3. In the midst of faults and fail - ures, Stand by
4. In the midst of per - se - cu - tion,
5. When I'm grow - ing old and fee - ble,
1. When the storms of life are rag - ing,
2. In the midst of trib - u - la - tions,
3. me, stand by me; In the midst of faults and fail - ures,
4. In the midst of per - se - cu - tion,
5. When I'm grow - ing old and fee - ble,
1. When the world is toss - ing me
2. When the hosts of hell as - sail,
3. Stand by me, stand by me; When I do the best I can,
4. When my foes in bat - tle ar - ray
5. When my life be-comes a bur - den,
1. Like a ship up - on the sea; Thou who
2. And my strength be - gins to fail, Thou who
3. And my friends mis - un - der - stand, Thou who
4. Un - der - take to stop my way, Thou who
5. And I'm near - ing chill - y Jor - dan, O thou

Words: Charles A. Tindley (1851-1933)
Music: Charles A. Tindley; harm. F. A. Clark

1. rul - est wind and wa - ter,
2. nev - er lost a bat - tle,
3. know - est all a - bout me, Stand by me. Stand by me.
4. saved Paul and Si - las,
5. "Lil - y of the Val - ley,"

’ve Got Peace Like a River

201

1. I’ve got peace like a riv - er, I’ve got peace like a
2. I’ve got joy like a foun-tain, I’ve got joy like a
3. I’ve got love like an o - cean, I’ve got love like an

1.

1. riv - er, I’ve got peace like a riv - er in my
2. foun - tain, I’ve got joy like a foun-tain in my
3. o - cean, I’ve got love like an o - cean in my

2.

1. soul; ________ I’ve got riv - er in my soul. ________
2. soul; ________ I’ve got foun - tain in my soul. ________
3. soul; ________ I’ve got o - cean in my soul. ________

’ords: Traditional
usic: Negro Spiritual

1. The church __ of __ God ____ must now pre - vail, a -
2. The church __ of __ God ____ must now pre - vail, no
3. The love ___ of __ God ____ must now pre - vail, Christ
4. The peace ___ of __ God ____ must now pre - vail, in
1. gainst the world's di - vi - sive scheme; The
2. breach de - form its sa - cred walls; When
3. spoke the love of Christ for all; And
4. Christ shall wars and ha - tred end; The
1. might - y strength of Un - ion pales, the
2. storms of hate and doubt as - sail, let
3. lov - ing God, love can - not fail, to
4. arms of earth can - not a - vail, the
1. ad - ver - sar - y of the ____ dream.
2. love and peace ____ reign in its ____ halls.
3. tran - scend ev' - ry ra - cial ____ wall.
4. peace of heav'n ____ a - lone can ____ win.

5. The reign of God must now prevail,
Let selfish strivings be undone;
Across the world His name we hail,
Our Lord and King, the risen son!

Words: C. Eric Lincoln (b. 1924). Used by Permission.
Music: Hezekiah Brinson, Jr. (b. 1958).

There Is a Balm in Gilead

There is a balm in Gil-e-ad to make the wound-ed
whole; There is a balm in Gil-e-ad to heal the sin-sick soul.
Fine
1. Some-times I feel dis-cour-aged, And think my work's in vain, But
2. If you can-not preach like Pet-er, If you can-not preach like Paul, You can
3. Don't ev-er be dis-cour-aged For Je-sus is your friend, And
1. then the ho-ly spir-it Re-vives my soul a-gain.
2. tell the love of Je-sus, And say He died for all.
3. if you lack for know-ledge, He'll ne'er re-fuse to lend.
D.C.

Words: Traditional
Music: American Melody; arr. Carl Haywood (b. 1949), from *The Haywood Collection of Negro Spirituals*,

Think of His Goodness to You

1. When waves of af - flic - tion sweep o - ver the soul,
2. The world may for - sake you, and those whom you trust
3. Mis - for - tune's dark cloud may hang o - ver the way,
4. When dear ones are tak - en a - way from you here,
1. And sun - light is hid - den from view, If
2. May prove to be false and un - true; There's
3. De - spite your best ef - forts to do; The
4. You loved with af - fec - tion so true, Look
1. ev - er you're tempt - ed to fret or com - plain, Just
2. one you can trust e - ven un - to the end; Just
3. sav - ior is guard - ing your treas - ures up there; Just
4. un - to the sav - ior for strength to en - dure, And
think of His good - ness to you.
think of His good - ness to you.
think of His good - ness to you.
think of His good - ness to you.

Words: R. C. Ward
Music: R. C. Ward

Just think of His good - ness to you;
His good - ness to you;
Yes, think of His good - ness to you;
His good - ness to you;
Though storms o'er thee sweep, He is a - ble to keep;
O think of His good - ness to you.

Trust and Obey

1. When we walk with the Lord In the light of His word, What a glo - ry He
2. Not a shad-ow can rise, Not a cloud in the skies, But His smile quick-ly
3. Not a bur-den we bear, Not a sor-row we share, But our toil He doth
4. But we nev - er can prove The de-lights of His love Un - til all on the
5. When in fel-low-ship sweet We will sit at His feet, Or we'll walk by His
1. sheds on our way! While we do His good will, He a - bides with us still,
2. drives it a - way; Not a doubt nor a fear, Not a sigh nor a tear,
3. rich - ly re - pay; Not a grief nor a loss, Not a frown nor a cross,
4. al - tar we lay; For the fav - or He shows, And the joy He be - stows,
5. side in the way; What He says we will do, Where He sends we will go,—
1. And with all who will trust and o - bey.
2. Can a - bide while we trust and o - bey.
3. But is blest if we trust and o - bey.
4. Are for them who will trust and o - bey.
5. Nev - er fear, on - ly trust and o - bey.
Trust and o - bey, for there's
no oth - er way To be hap - py in Je - sus, But to trust and o - bey.

Words: J. H. Sammis
Music: D. B. Towner

1. We walk by faith, and not by sight;
2. We may not touch His hands and side,
3. Help then, O Lord, our un - be - lief;
4. That, when our life of faith is done;
1. no gra - cious words we hear from Him who
2. nor fol - low where He trod; but in His
3. and may our faith a - bound, to call on
4. in realms of clear - er light, we may be -
1. spoke as none e'er spoke; but we be -
2. prom - ise we re - joice, and cry, "My
3. you when you are near, and seek where
4. hold you as you are, with full and
1.,2.,3.
4.
1. lieve Him near.
2. Lord and God!"
3. you are found.
4. end - less sight.

'ords: Henry Alford (1810-1871)
lusic: Eugene W. Hancock (b. 1929)

We'll Understand It Better By and By

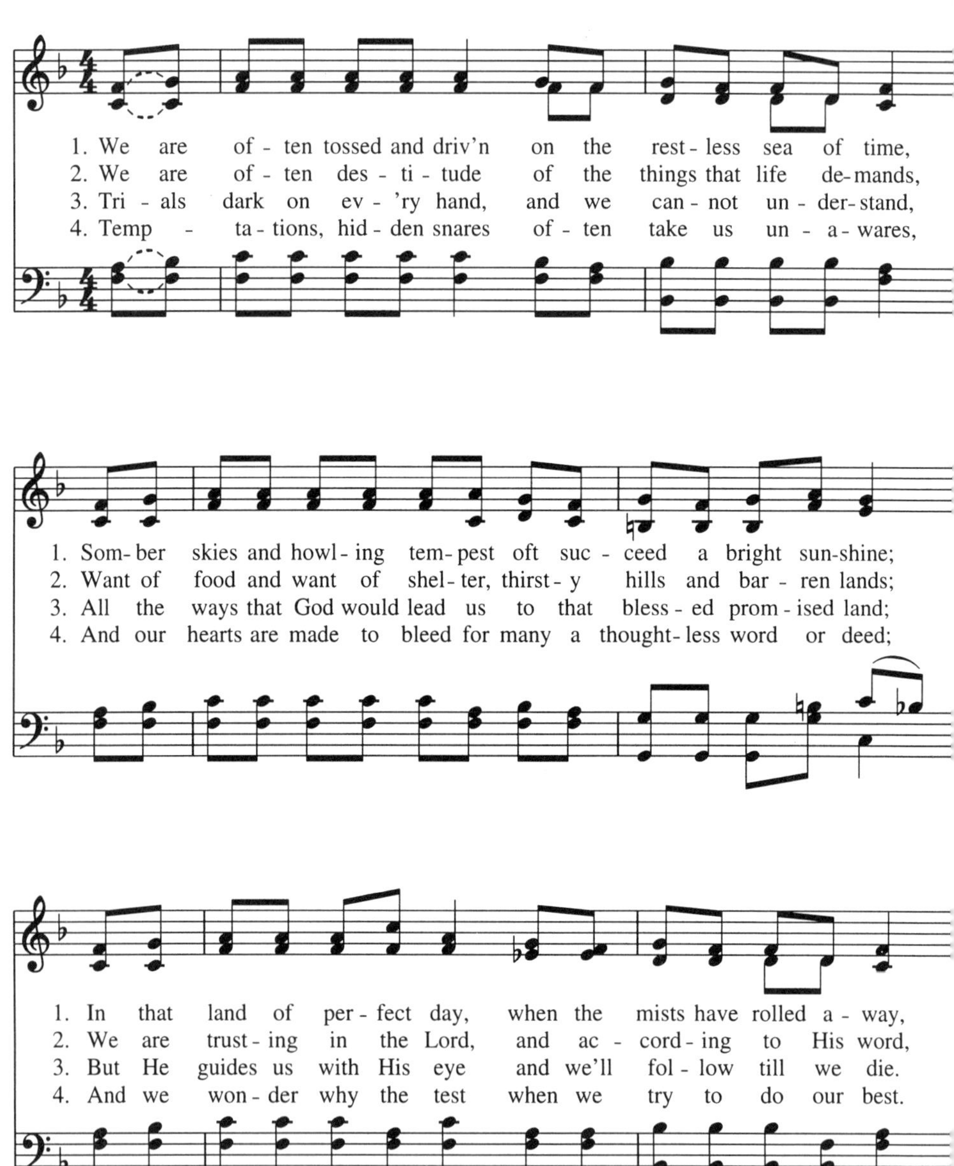
1. We are of - ten tossed and driv'n on the rest - less sea of time,
2. We are of - ten des - ti - tude of the things that life de-mands,
3. Tri - als dark on ev - 'ry hand, and we can - not un - der-stand,
4. Temp - ta - tions, hid - den snares of - ten take us un - a - wares,
1. Som-ber skies and howl - ing tem-pest oft suc - ceed a bright sun-shine;
2. Want of food and want of shel-ter, thirst - y hills and bar - ren lands;
3. All the ways that God would lead us to that bless - ed prom - ised land;
4. And our hearts are made to bleed for many a thought-less word or deed;
1. In that land of per - fect day, when the mists have rolled a - way,
2. We are trust - ing in the Lord, and ac - cord - ing to His word,
3. But He guides us with His eye and we'll fol - low till we die.
4. And we won - der why the test when we try to do our best.

Words: Charles A. Tindley (1851-1933)
Music: Charles A. Tindley; arr. F. A. Clark, c. 1906

1. We will
2. We will
3. For we'll
4. But we'll
un - der-stand it bet - ter by and by, by and by.
By and by ___ when the morn-ing comes, When the saints of
God are gath - ered home, We'll tell the sto - ry
how we're o - ver - come; For we'll un - der - stand it bet - ter by and by, by and by.

Refrain
We've come this far by faith,
Leaning on the Lord;
Trusting in His holy word,
He's never failed me yet.
O

Words: Albert A. Goodson
Music: Albert A. Goodson; harm. Richard Smallwood

Fine
can't turn a - round. We've come this far by faith.
1. Don't be dis-cour-aged when trou-ble's in your life. He'll bear your
bur - dens and move all mis - er - y and strife. That's why we've
D.S.

2. Just the other day I heard someone say
He didn't believe in God's word;
But I can truly say that God had made a way
And He never failed me yet.
That's why we've (Refrain)

Yes, God Is Real

There are some things I may not know, these are some
There are some things I may not know,
plac - es I can't go; But I am sure of this one
There are plac - es I can't go; But I am sure
thing, that God is real for I can feel Him deep with -
of this one thing, God is real He's

Words: Kenneth Morris (1917–1988)
Music: Kenneth Morris (1917–1988); arr. Horace Clarence Boyer (b. 1935)

in. Yes, God is real, real in my
deep with-in my soul. Yes, God is real,
soul. Yes, God is real, for He has washed and made me
real in my soul. real, for He has washed and made me
whole; His love for me is like pure
whole; His love for me
gold, Yes, God is real, for I can feel Him in my soul.
is like pure gold, real, I feel Him deep with-in my soul.

1. Goin' to lay down my sword and shield,
2. Goin' to lay down my war ___ shoes,
3. Goin' to put on my long white robe,
4. Goin' to meet my lov - ing sav - ior,

Down by the riv - er - side, Down by the riv - er - side,

Down by the riv - er - side.

1. Goin' to lay down my sword and shield,
2. Goin' to lay down my war ___ shoes,
3. Goin' to put on my long white robe,
4. Goin' to meet my lov - ing sav - ior,

Down by the riv - er - side, To stud - y war ___ no

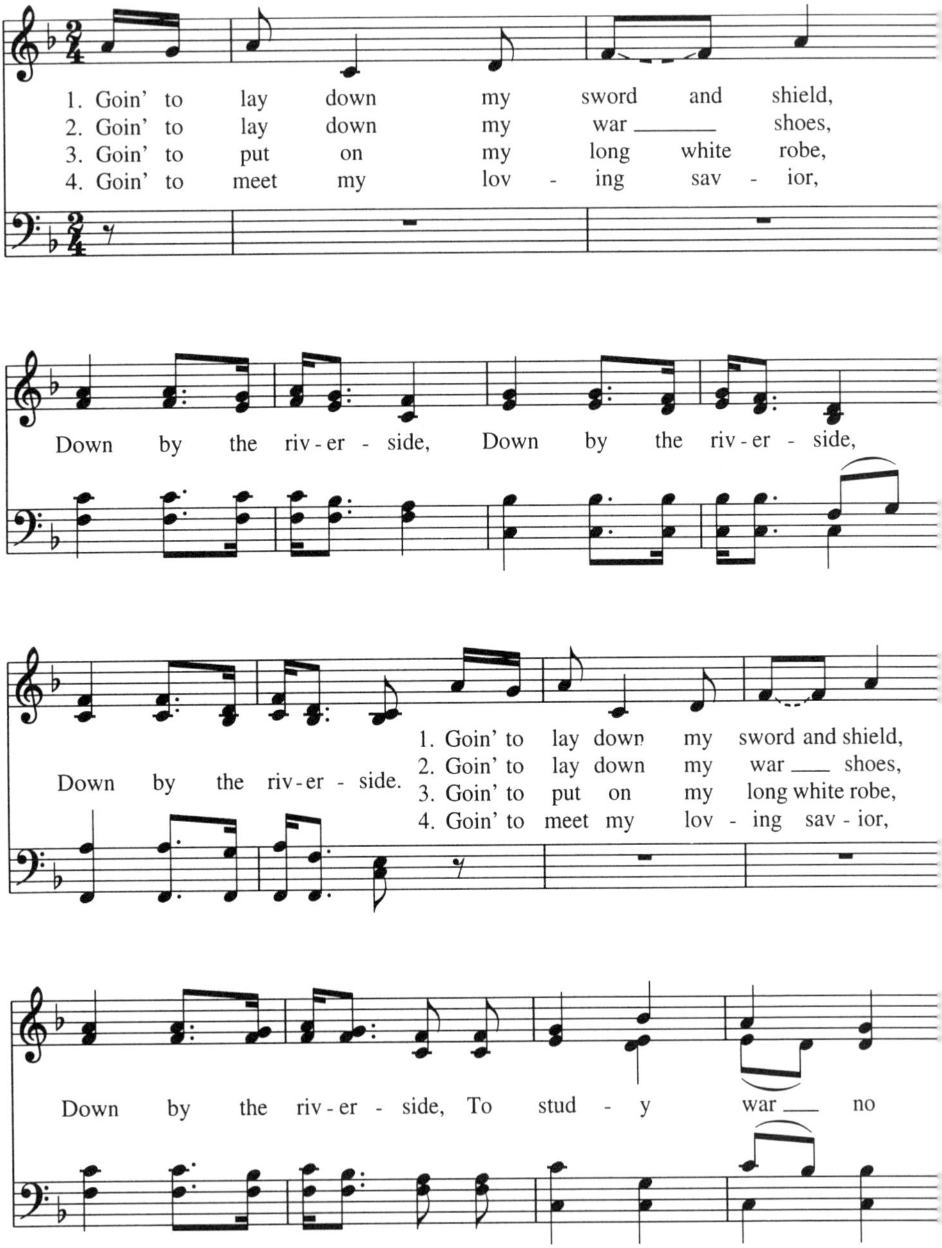

Words: Traditional
Music: Negro Spiritual; arr. Clarence C. White

I ain't goin't
more.
stud - y war no more, Ain't goin't
stud - y war no more, Ain't goin't stud - y war no
war,
I ain't goin't
more,
stud - y war no more, Ain't goin't
stud-y war no more,
stud-y war no more, Ain't goin't stud - y war no more.

211 **Little David, Play on Your Harp**

Lit-tle Da-vid, play on your harp, Hal - le - lu! Hal - le -

1.
2.
Fin
lu! Lit-tle Da-vid, play on your harp, Hal - le - lu! Lit-tle Da-vid. lu!

1. Lit - tle Da - vid was a shep-herd boy, He
2. O Josh - u - a was the son of Nun, He

D.C
1. killed Go - li - ath and shout - ed for joy.
2. nev - er would quit till the work was done.

Words: Traditional
Music: Negro Spiritual

Born to Rule the Earth

1. Born to rule the earth, Born to rule the sky, Born to rule the world To
walk up-on the sea, Lit-tle boy, lit-tle boy.
2. Je-sus rule the earth, Je-sus rule the sky, Je-sus rule the world and
walk up-on the sea, Lit-tle boy, lit-tle boy.
3. Born to rule the earth, Born to rule the sky, Born to rule the world To
res-cue you and me, What a joy, Lit-tle boy, What a joy.

Words: Traditional, Jamaica
Music: Traditional, Jamaica; arr. Edward Henry

213 Children of the Heavenly Father

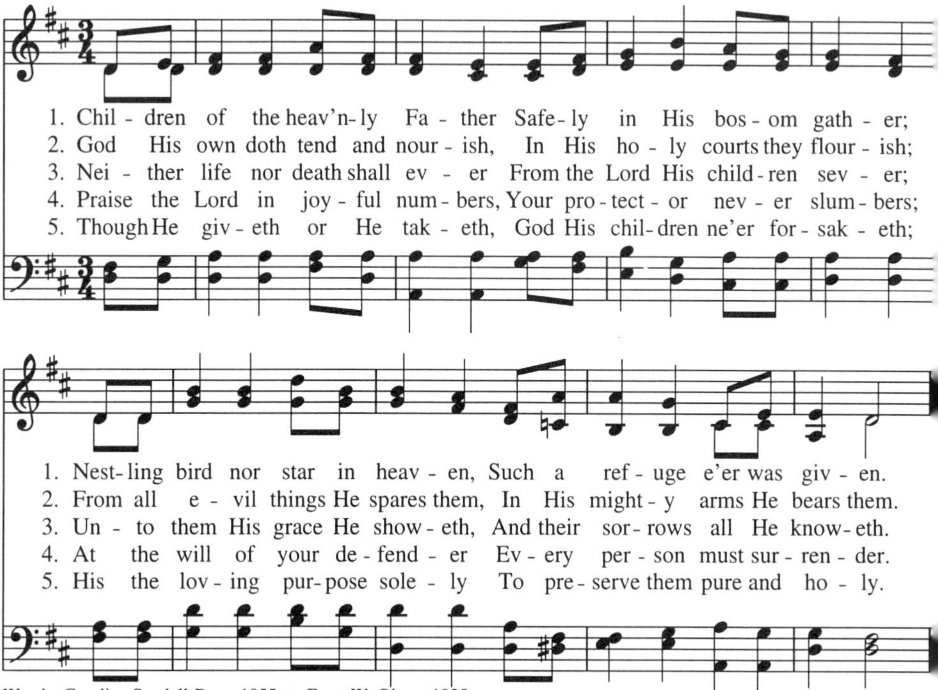

1. Children of the heav'nly Father Safely in His bosom gather;
Nestling bird nor star in heaven, Such a refuge e'er was given.

2. God His own doth tend and nourish, In His holy courts they flourish;
From all evil things He spares them, In His mighty arms He bears them.

3. Neither life nor death shall ever From the Lord His children sever;
Unto them His grace He showeth, And their sorrows all He knoweth.

4. Praise the Lord in joyful numbers, Your protector never slumbers;
At the will of your defender Every person must surrender.

5. Though He giveth or He taketh, God His children ne'er forsaketh;
His the loving purpose solely To preserve them pure and holy.

Words: Carolina Sandell-Berg, 1855; tr. Ernst W. Olson, 1925
Music: Swedish Folk Melody

214 God Is So Good

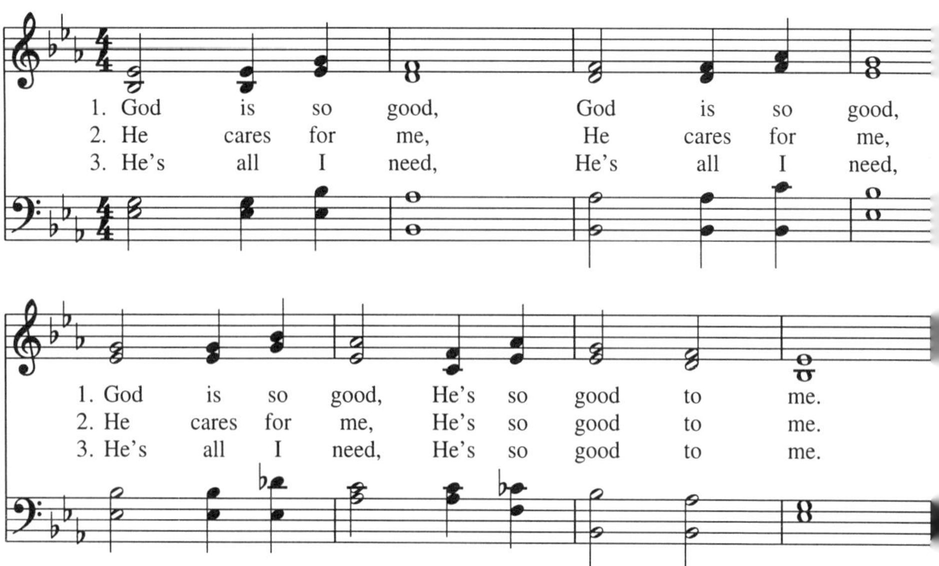
1. God is so good, God is so good,
2. He cares for me, He cares for me,
3. He's all I need, He's all I need,
1. God is so good, He's so good to me.
2. He cares for me, He's so good to me.
3. He's all I need, He's so good to me.

Words: Traditional
Music: Negro Spiritual

Great Are You, O Lord

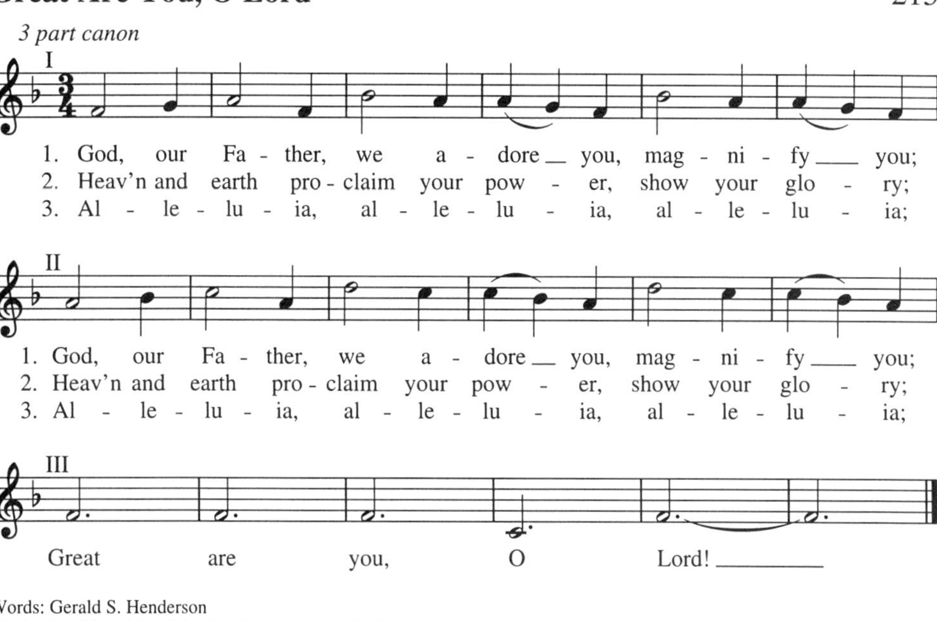
3 part canon
I
1. God, our Fa - ther, we a - dore ___ you, mag - ni - fy ___ you;
2. Heav'n and earth pro - claim your pow - er, show your glo - ry;
3. Al - le - lu - ia, al - le - lu - ia, al - le - lu - ia;
II
1. God, our Fa - ther, we a - dore ___ you, mag - ni - fy ___ you;
2. Heav'n and earth pro - claim your pow - er, show your glo - ry;
3. Al - le - lu - ia, al - le - lu - ia, al - le - lu - ia;
III
Great are you, O Lord! ___

Words: Gerald S. Henderson
Music: Traditional English Melody; arr. Gerald S. Henderson

In My Life, Lord, Be Glorified

1. In my life, Lord, be glo - ri - fied, ___ be glo - ri - fied; ___
2. In my song, Lord, be glo - ri - fied, ___ be glo - ri - fied; ___
3. In your church, Lord, be glo - ri - fied, ___ be glo - ri - fied; ___
1. In my life, Lord, be glo - ri - fied ___ to - day.
2. In my song, Lord, be glo - ri - fied ___ to - day.
3. In your church, Lord, be glo - ri - fied ___ to - day.

Words: Bob Kilpatrick (b. 1952)
Music: Bob Kilpatrick

He's Got the Whole World in His Hand

1. He's got the whole world in His hand, He's got the

whole world in His hand, He's got the whole world

in His hand, He's got the whole world in His hand.

2. He's got you and me sister, etc.
3. He's got you and me brother, etc.
4. He's got the pretty little baby, etc.
5. He's got everybody here, etc.

Words: Traditional
Music: Negro Spiritual; arr. Hezekiah Brinson, Jr. (b. 1958)

Jesus Loves Me, This I Know

1. Je - sus loves me! this I know, For the bi - ble tells me so;
2. Je - sus loves me! He who died, Hea - ven's gate to op - en wide;
3. Je - sus take this heart of mine, Make it pure and whol - ly thine;
1. Lit - tle ones to Him be - long; They are weak but He is strong.
2. He will wash a - way my sin, Let His lit - tle child come in.
3. On the cross you died for me, I will try to live for thee.
Yes, Je - sus loves me! Yes, Je - sus loves me!
Yes, Je - sus loves me! The bi - ble tells me so.

Words: Traditional; Anne B. Warner (1820-1915)
Music: William B. Bradbury (1816-1869); arr. Horace Clarence Boyer (b. 1935)

This Is the Day

This is the day, this is the day that the Lord hath made, that the
Lord hath made, we will re-joice, we will re-joice and be
glad in it, and be glad in it; This is the day that the
Lord hath made, we will re-joice and be glad in it;
This is the day, this is the day that the Lord hath made.

Words: Psalm 118:24
Music: Les Garrett

We Are Climbing Jacob's Ladder

220

1. We are climb - ing Ja - cob's lad - der,
2. Ev' ry' round goes high - er, high - er,
3. Sin - ner do you love your Je - sus?
4. If you love Him why not serve Him,
1. We are climb - ing Ja - cob's lad - der;
2. Ev' ry' round goes high - er, high - er;
3. Sin - ner do you love your Je - sus?
4. If you love Him why not serve Him;
1. We are climb - ing Ja - cob's lad - der,
2. Ev' ry' round goes high - er, high - er,
3. Sin - ner do you love your Je - sus?
4. If you love Him why not serve Him,
1. Sol - diers of the cross.
2. Sol - diers of the cross.
3. Sol - diers of the cross.
4. Sol - diers of the cross.

Words: Traditional
Music: Negro Spiritual; arr. Horace Clarence Boyer (b. 1935)

This Little Light of Mine

1. This lit - tle light of mine, I'm gon - na let it shine, This lit - tle light of mine, I'm gon - na let it shine; This lit - tle light of mine, I'm gon - na let it shine, Let it
2. Ev - 'ry - where I go, I'm gon - na let it shine, Ev - 'ry - where I go, I'm gon - na let it shine; Ev - 'ry - where I go, I'm gon - na let it shine, Let it
3. Je - sus gave it to me, I'm gon - na let it shine, Je - sus gave it to me, I'm gon - na let it shine; Je - sus gave it to me, I'm gon - na let it shine, Let it
Oh
Oh
Oh
Oh

Words: Traditional
Music: Negro Spiritual; arr. Horace Clarence Boyer (b. 1935)

1. shine, let it shine, let it shine.
2. shine, let it shine, let it shine.
3. shine, let it shine, let it shine.

Jesus Loves the Little Children

222

Je - sus loves the lit - tle chil - dren, All the chil - dren of the world;
Red and yel - low, black and white, They are pre - cious in His sight,
Je - sus loves the lit - tle chil - dren of the world.

Words: Anonymous
Music: George F. Root (1820-1895)

Joshua Fit de Battle of Jericho

Josh - ua fit de bat - tle of Jer - i - cho, Jer - i - cho,
Jer - i - cho; Josh - ua fit de bat - tle of Jer - i - cho, An' de
walls come tum - blin' down.
1. Fine 2.
1. You may
talk a - bout the man of Gid - e - on, You may talk a - bout the man of

Words: Traditional
Music: Negro Spiritual; arr. Irma Tillery (b. 1925). Used by Permission.

Saul; Dere's none like good ole Josh - ua, an' de
bat - tle of Jer - i - cho. 2. Up to the walls of
Jer - i - cho, He marched with spear in hand; "Go
D.C.
blow dem ram horns," Josh - ua cried, "for the bat - tle am in my hand." Oh

E - ze-k'el saw de wheel 'Way up in de mid-dle o' de air, E - ze-k'el saw de
wheel 'Way in de mid-dle o' de air. De big wheel run by faith, De lit-tle wheel run
by de Grace o' God, A wheel in a wheel 'Way in de mid-dle o' de air.
Fin
1. Bet-ter min', my sis - ter, how you walk on de cross,
2. Let me tell you, broth - er, what a sin - ner will do, 'Way in de mid - dle o' de
air, Yo' foot might slip an' yo' soul be los'. 'Way in de mid - dle o' de air.
He'll step on you an' he'll step on me.
D.C

Words: Traditional
Music: Negro Spiritual; harm. J. Jefferson Cleveland (1937-1988)

Oh, Freedom!

225

1. Oh, free - dom! Oh, free - dom, Oh, free - dom o - ver me! An' be fo' I'd be a slave I'll be bur - ied in my grave, An' go home to my Lord an' be free.
2. No mo' moan - in', no mo' moan-in', no mo' moan - in' o - ver me! An' be fo' I'd be a slave I'll be bur - ied in my grave, An' go home to my Lord an' be free.

3. No mo' weepin'...
4. There'll be singin'...
5. There'll be shoutin'...
6. There'll be prayin'...

Words: Traditional
Music: Negro Spiritual; arr. Carl Haywood (b. 1949), from *The Haywood Collection of Negro Spirituals*,

226 Mine Eyes Have Seen the Glory

1. Mine ___ eyes have seen the glo - ry of the
2. I have seen Him in the watch - fires of a
3. He has sound - ed forth the trum - et that shall
4. In the beau - ty of the lil - ies, Christ was
1. com - ing of the Lord; He is tram - pling out the vin - tage where the
2. hund - red cir - cling camps, They have build - ed Him an al - tar in the
3. nev - er sound re - treat, He is sift - ing out the hearts of men be -
4. born a - cross the sea, With a glo - ry in His bos - om that trans -
1. grapes of wrath are stored; He has loosed the fate - ful light - ning of His
2. eve - ning dews and damps; I can read His right - eous sent - ence by the
3. fore His judge - ment seat; O be swift, my soul, to an - swer Him! be
4. fig - ures you and me; As He died to make men ho - ly, let us
1. ter - ri - ble swift sword, His truth is march - ing on.
2. dim and flar - ing lamps, His day is march - ing on.
3. ju - bi - lant, my feet! Our God is march - ing on.
4. live to make all free, While God is march - ing on.

Words: Jula W. Howe (1819-1910)
Music: *Battle Hymn of the Republic*, William Steffe; arr. Horace Clarence Boyer (b. 1935)

Glo - ry, glo - ry, hal - le - lu - jah!
Glo - ry, glo - ry, hal - le - lu - jah! Glo - ry, glo - ry, hal - le
lu - jah! His truth is march - ing on.

We Shall Overcome

We shall o - ver - come, We shall o - ver come,
we shall o - ver - come some - day; Oh,
deep in my heart, I do be - lieve,
(Oh)
1.- 4.
5.
We shall o - ver - come some - day. day.

2. We'll walk hand in hand, today.
3. God is on our side, today.
4. We are not afraid, today.
5. We shall live in peace, someday.

Words: Traditional
Music: Negro Spiritual; arr. Carl Haywood (b. 1949), from *The Haywood Collection of Negro Spirituals*,

Go Down, Moses

228

1. When Is - rael was in E-gypt's land, let my peo - ple go;
2. The Lord told Mo - ses what to do, let my peo - ple go;
3. They jour-neyed on at his com - mand, let my peo - ple go;
4. Oh, let us all from bond-age flee, let my peo - ple go;
1. op - pressed so hard they could not stand, let my peo - ple go.
2. to lead the chil-dren of Is - rael through, let my peo - ple go.
3. and came at length to Ca-naan's land, let my peo - ple go.
4. and let us all in Christ be free, let my peo - ple go.
Go down, Mo - ses, way down in E - gypt's land;
tell old Pha - roah to let my peo-ple go.

Words: Traditional
Music: Negro Spiritual; arr. Horace Clarence Boyer (b. 1935)

Keep the Dream Alive

Mar-tin's dream for all of us so set his soul a - fire, And
lift - ed him to soar - ing heights that he might with his God con -
spire; To change the course of his - to - ry that all be bro-thers,

Words: Robert Manuel, Sr.
Music: Hezekiah Brinson, Jr. (b. 1958).

Free at Last 230

all be free. Keep the dream a - live, Keep the dream a -
live; We will have the vic - to - ry, Just
1. keep the dream a - live. We'll
2. keep the dream a - live.
We will
Free at last, free at last, I thank God I'm
free at last, Free at last, free at last,

Words: Traditional
Music: Negro Spiritual; arr. John W. Work (1901-1967)
Arr. used by permission of Mrs. J. W. Work.

1.
2.
Fine
I thank God I'm free at last. O free at last.
1. 'Way down yonder in the grave-yard walk, I thank God I'm
2. On - a my knees when the light pass'd by, I thank God I'm
3. Some of these morn - ings, bright and fair, I thank God I'm
1. free at last, Me and my Je - sus goin' to
2. free at last, Tho't my soul would
3. free at last, Goin' meet King Je - sus
D.C.
1. meet and talk, I thank God I'm free at last, O
2. rise and fly, I thank God I'm free at last, O
3. in the air, I thank God I'm free at last,

A Choral Benediction

231

The Lord bless you and keep you: The Lord make his face to shine upon you, And be gracious unto you, The Lord lift up His countenance upon you, And give you peace. A -

And be

A -

A -

Words: Numbers 6:24-26
Music: Carl Haywood (b. 1949), from *Songs of Praise*, Copyright ©1992.

- men, A - men, A - men.
- men, A - men, A - men.
- men, A - men, A - men.

232 Thank You, Lord

Thank you, Lord, Thank you,
Lord; Thank you, Lord
I just want to thank you, Lord.

Words: Traditional
Music: Negro Spiritual; arr. Hezekiah Brinson, Jr. (b. 1958)

A - men, A - men,
Lordy - y good Lord - y
1. See the lit - tle ba - by
A - men, A - men, A - men,
1. Ly - ing in a man-ger On Christ - mas morn - ing.
2. Talk-ing to the eld - ers, They mar-v'ld at His wis - dom.
3. Pray-ing to his fa - ther As Ju - das be-trays Him.
4. Dy - ing for us sin-ners but He rose on Eas - ter.
A - men, A - men,
1.,2.,3.
4.
2. See Him in the tem - ple,
3. See Him in the gar - den,
4. See Him there at Cal - v'ry,
A - men, A - men, A - men.
men.

Words: Traditional
Music: Negro Spiritual; arr. Horace Clarence Boyer (b. 1935)

God Be With You

God be with you,
God be with you,
God be with you, until we meet again;
God be with you,
God be with you,
God be with you, until we meet again.

Words: Thomas A. Dorsey (1899-1993)
Music: Tomas A. Dorsey; arr. Horace Clarence Boyer (b. 1935)

Service Music

KYRIE

235 **Lord, Have Mercy**

Lord have mer - cy, Lord have mer - cy, Lord have

Fine
mer - cy. Christ have mer - cy,
Fine

Music: Lena McLin, *Eucharist of the Soul*
Reprinted from *Eucharist of the Soul* (GC41)

D.C.
Christ have mer - cy, Christ have mer - cy.
D.C.

Lord, Have Mercy

236

Lord, have mer - cy, Lord, have

mer - cy, Lord, have ner - cy on

Music: Leon C. Roberts (1950-1999), *Mass of St. Augustine.*

us.
Christ,
have

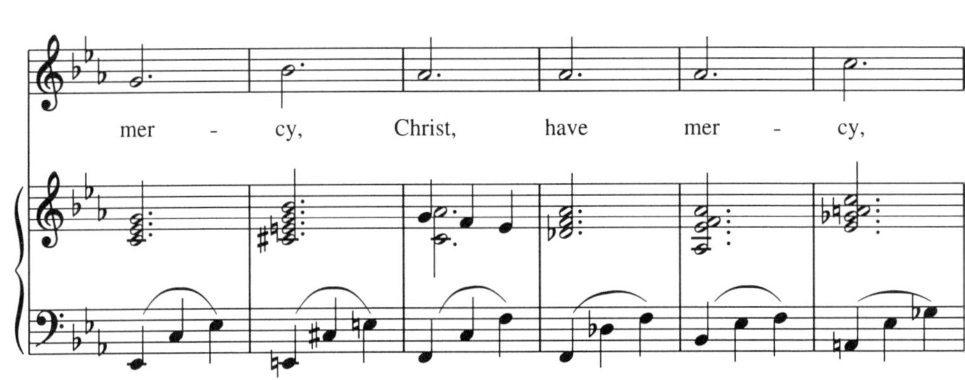
mer - cy,
Christ,
have
mer - cy,

Christ,
have
mer - cy
on
us.

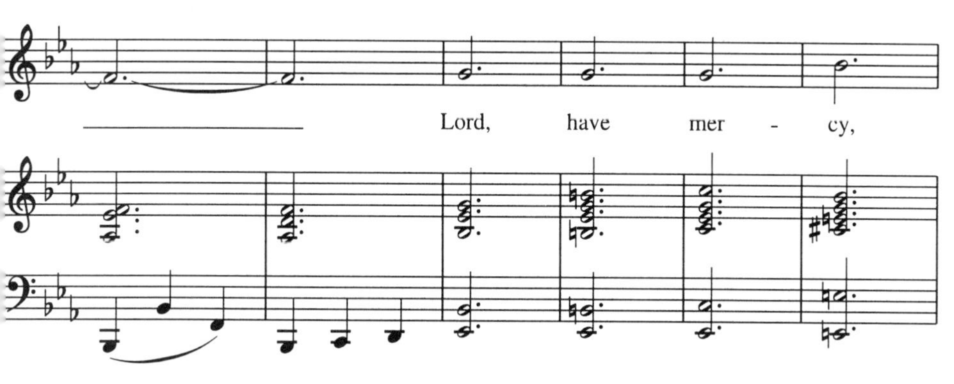

Lord, have mer - cy,

Lord, have mer - cy, Lord, have

mer - cy, have mer - cy on us.

237 Lord, Have Mercy

Lord, have mer - cy, Christ, have mer - cy.
Lord, have mer - cy, have mer - cy, O, Lord.

Music: Avon Gillespie (1937-1989), *Mass No. 1 in G*

238 Lord, Have Mercy / Kyrie Eleison

Lord, have mer - cy. Christ, have mer - cy. Lord, have mer - cy.

Ky - ri - e e - le - i - son. Chri - ste, e - le - i - son. Ky - ri - e e - le - i - son.

Music: William B. Cooper

Kyrie Eleison

239

Leader

Ky - ri - e

Ky-ri - e e - le - i - son. Ky-ri -

Christ - te

e e - le - i - son. Christ - te e - le - i -

Ky - ri - e

son. Chris - te e - le - i - son. Ky-ri -

e e - le - i - son. Ky-ri - e e - le - i - son.

Music: Betty Carr Pulkingham (b. 1928), *Freedom Mass*. Based on traditional African melodies.

Lord, have mer - cy, Have mer - cy, have mer - cy! Lord,
have mer - cy, Have mer - cy, have mer - cy. Lord,
have mer - cy, Have mer - cy, have mer - cy! Lord,
have mer - cy.

Music: Garfield Rochard

GLORIA

Glory to God

241

Glo - ry to God in the high-est, and
peace to His peo - ple on earth.
Lord God, heav-en-ly King, al - might - y God and Fa - ther,

Music: David Hurd (b. 1950), *Intercession Mass*

we worship you, we give you thanks, we
praise you for your glory.
Lord Jesus Christ, only
Son of the Father,
Sw.
Gt.

Lord God, Lamb of God, you take a - way the sin of the
Sw.
Man.
world: have mer-cy on us;
Gt.
Sw.
Gt.
Ped.
you are seat-ed at the right hand of the Fa - ther: re - ceive our
prayer. For
Gt.

you a-lone are the Ho-ly One, you a-lone are the Lord,
you a-lone are the Most High,
Je - sus Christ, with the Ho-ly Spir-it, in the
glo-ry of God the Fa-ther. A - men.

Leader
All
Glo - ry to God in the high - est, And peace to His
peo - ple on earth. Lord God, heav'n - ly King,
Al - migh-ty God, and Fa - ther,
we wor-ship you,
we give you thanks, we praise you for your glo - - ry.

Music: Lena McLin, *Eucharist of the Soul*
Reprinted from *Eucharist of the Soul* (GC41)

Lord Je-sus Christ, on-ly Son of the Fa-ther, Lord God, Lamb of God, you
take a-way the sin of the world: have mer-cy on us;
5
You are seat-ed at the right hand of the Fa-ther: re-ceive
our prayer. For you a-lone are the

Ho - ly One, you a - lone are the Lord, you a -
lone are the Most High, Je - sus Christ, with the Ho - ly Spir - it, in the
glo - ry of God _ the Fa - ther. A - men. A -
men. A - men. A - men.

Glory to God

Glo - ry,
Glo-ry, hal - le- lu - jah, Lord we praise your Ho - ly name, Glo-ry,
Glo - ry ha - le- lu - jah, Lord we praise your Ho - ly name.

1. Glo-ry to God in the high - est and peace to His peo - ple on earth.
2. Lord God, heav-en-ly King, al - might - y God and Fa - ther, we
wor - ship you, we give you thanks, we praise you for your glo - ry.

Unison
3. Lord Je-sus Christ, on-ly son of the Fa - ther, Lord God, Lamb of God, Glo-ry,
Glo-ry, hal-le-lu - jah, Lord we praise your Ho - ly name, Glo-ry,
Glo-ry ha-le-lu - jah, Lord we praise your Ho - ly name. 4. You

take a-way the sin of the world: have mer - cy on us, 5. You are
seat-ed at the right hand of the Fa - ther: re - ceive our prayer. 6. For
you a-lone are the Ho - ly One, You a - lone are the Lord,

Unison
7. You a-lone _ are the Most High, Je - sus Christ, with the Ho - ly Spi-rit, in the
Descant
Lord, _______ Lord _ we
glo - ry of _ the Fa - ther. Glo - ry, Glo - ry, hal - le - lu - jah, Lord we
praise __________ you _______ Lord, _______ Lord _ hal - le -
praise your Ho - ly name, _ Glo - ry, Glo - ry ha - le - lu - jah, Lord we

Descant
lu - jah.
Women
Praise your Ho - ly name.
Men
Praise your Ho - ly name.
A - - - - - - men.

SONGS OF PRAISE

244

I Will Rejoic

I will re - joice,
I will be glad,
I will praise God Who holds my life,

Words: Grayson Warren Brown (b. 1948)
Music: Grayson Warren Brown; harm. Larry Adams

in His hands.
I will re - joice,
1.
2.
1. I will praise the Fa - ther,
2. I will praise the Fa - ther,
1. I will praise the Son.
2. each and ev' - ry day
and I will praise the Spir -
I will sing His love

1. - it for - ev - er more.
2. songs for - ev - er more.
I will re - joice,
I will re - joice,
1.
2.
I will be glad,
I will be glad,
I will praise God, Who holds my life in His hands.
D.S.
D.S.

Ve Have Come Into His House

1. We have come in - to His house and gath - ered in His name to
2. So for - get a - bout your - self and con - cen - trate on Him and
3. Let us lift up ho - ly hands and mag - ni - fy His name and
1. wor - ship Him, We have come in - to His house and
2. wor - ship Him, So for - get a - bout your - self and
3. wor - ship Him, Let us lift up ho - ly hands and
1. gath-ered in His name to wor - ship Him; We have
2. con - cen-trate on Him and wor - ship Him; So for -
3. mag - ni - fy His name and wor - ship Him; Let us
1. come in - to His house and gath - ered in His name to
2. get a - bout your - self and con - cen - trate on Him and
3. lift up ho - ly hands and mag - ni - fy His name and
wor-ship Christ, the Lord, Wor-ship Him, Christ the Lord.

Vords: Bruce Ballinger (b. 1945)
Iusic: Bruce Ballinger

Praise, Honor, and Glory

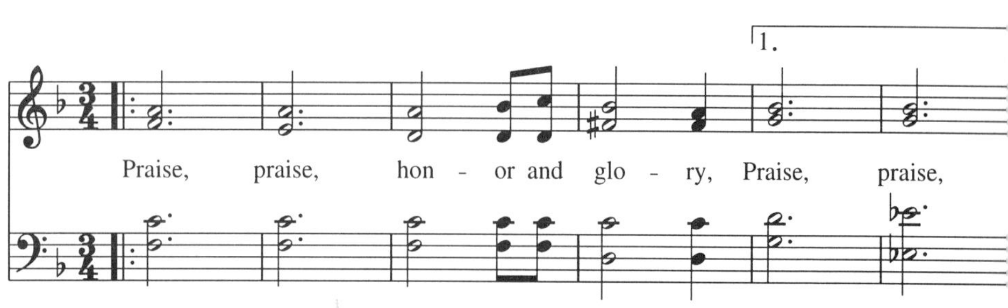
1.
Praise, praise, hon - or and glo - ry, Praise, praise,

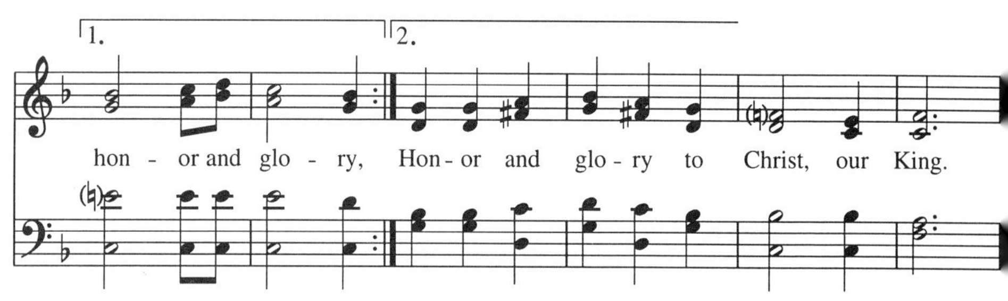
1.
2.
hon - or and glo - ry, Hon - or and glo - ry to Christ, our King.

Words: Don Sasser
Music: Don Sasser

PRAYERS OF THE PEOPLE AND RESPONSES

The Prayers of the People: Form I

247

Leader

With all our heart and with all our mind, let us pray to the Lord,

Say - ing "Lord, have _ mer - cy.

Leader

* For . . . . . , let us pray to the Lord.

People

Lord, have ___ mer - cy.

(This response is sung after each petition)

Leader Concludes

In the communion of [________________ and of all the] saints, let us commend

ourselves, and one an- o- ther, and all our life, to Christ our God.

People

To thee, / you, O Lord our God. A - men.

**The complete text is located in The Book of Common Prayer.*

Music: Carl Haywood (b. 1949), from *Mass for Grace*, Copyright © 1992.

Leader:
Let us pray for the Church and for the world.

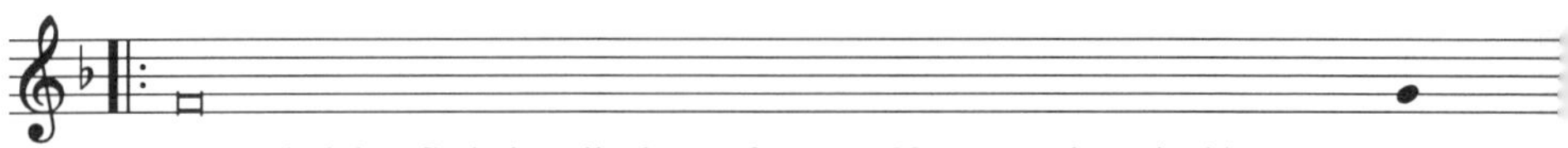

Grant, Almighty God, that all who confess your Name may be united in your truth, live together in your love, and reveal your glory in the world. *Response*

Guide the people of this land, and of all the nations, in the ways of justice and peace; that we may honor one another and serve the common good. *Response*

Give us all a reverence for the earth as your own creation, that we may use its resources rightly in the service of others and to your honor and glory. *Response*

Bless all whose lives are closely linked with ours, and grant that we may serve Christ in them, and love one another as he loves us. *Response*

Comfort and heal all those who suffer in body, mind, or spirit; give them courage and hope in their troubles, and bring them the joy of your salvation. *Response*

We commend to your mercy all who have died, that your will for them may be fulfilled; and we pray that we may share with all your saints in your eternal kingdom. *Response*

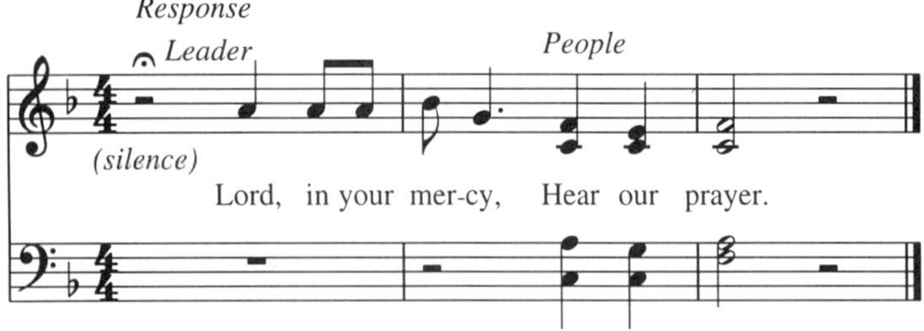
Response
Leader
People
(silence)
Lord, in your mer-cy, Hear our prayer.

Music: Betty Carr Pulkingham (b. 1928), *Freedom Mass*. Based on traditional African melodies.

Hear Our Prayer, O Lord

Hear our prayer, O Lord, hear our prayer, O Lord; In - cline thine ear to us, and grant us thy peace.

Words: George Whelpton (1847-1930)
Music: George Whelpton

O Lord, Hear Us We Pray

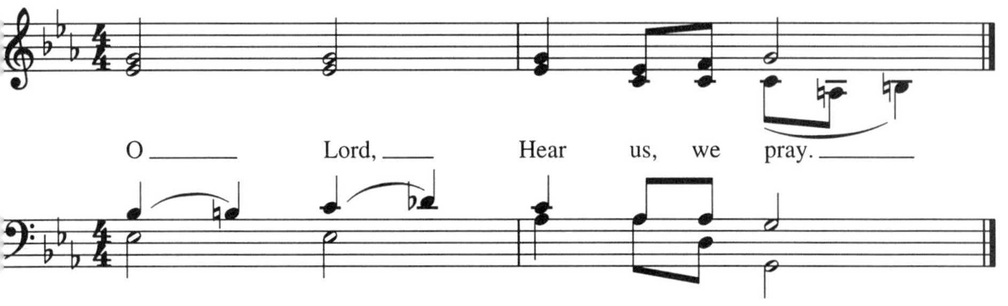
O Lord, Hear us, we pray.

Words: James E. Moore, Jr.
Music: James E. Moore, Jr.

251 **Lead Me, Lord**

Lead me, Lord, lead me in thy right - eous-ness,

Make thy way plain be - fore thy face. A - men.

Words: Psalm 5:8, 4:8
Music: Samuel S. Wesley (1861-1935)

SANCTUS

252 **Holy, Holy, Holy**

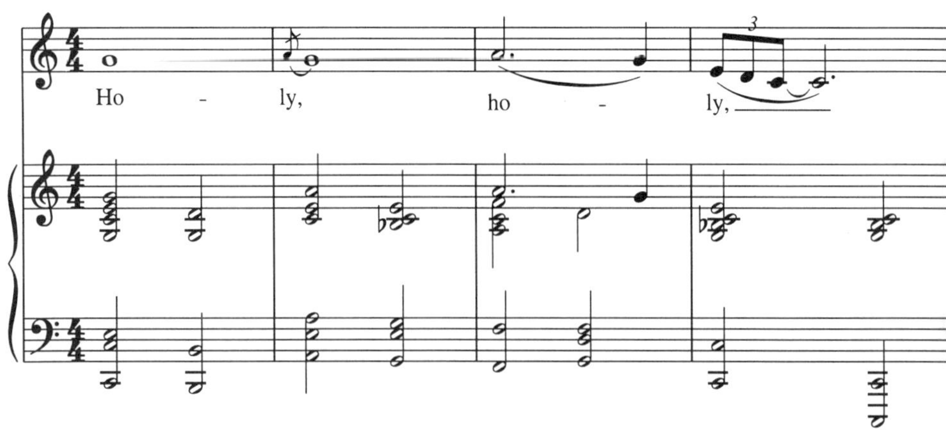
Ho - ly, ho - ly,

Music: Lena McLin, *Eucharist of the Soul*
Reprinted from *Eucharist of the Soul* (GC41)

ho - ly Lord, God of power and might,
heaven and earth are full of your glo - ry Ho - san-na in the
high - est. Bless - ed is he who comes in the name of the
Lord. Ho - san-na in the high - est.

Holy, Holy, Holy

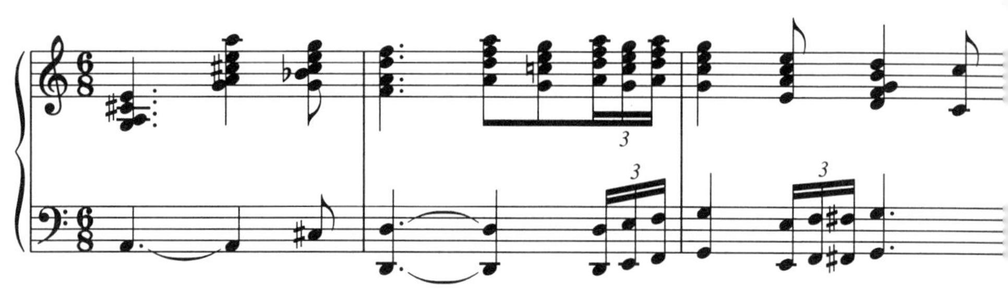

Ho - ly,

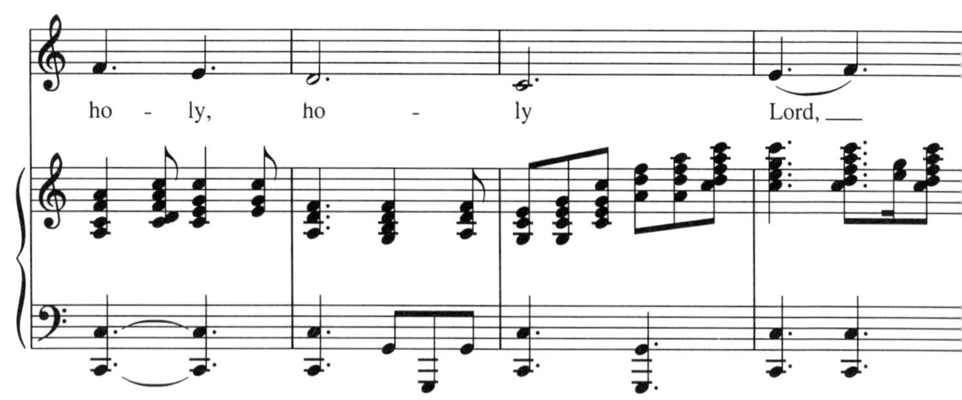
ho - ly, ho - ly Lord, ___

Music: Grayson Warren Brown (b. 1948); arr. Val Parker

God of pow - er and might,
1. Heav - en and earth are full
2.,3. Bless - ed is he who comes
1. of your glo - ry.
2.3. in the name of the Lord.
1.,2.
Ho - san - na! Ho - san -

na in the high -
est.
3.
san - na, Ho -
san - na in the high - est.

Ho - ly,
Ho - ly,
Ho - ly Lord,
God of pow - er and might,
Heav - en and earth are full of your

Music: Carl MaultsBy, *The Saint Mary Mass*

glo - ry. Ho - san - na in the
high-est. Bless-ed is he who
comes in the name of the Lord. Ho - san - na
in the high-est.

Holy, Holy, Holy

Ho - ly, ho - ly, ho - ly, ho - ly,
ho - ly Lord God of hosts.

Music: Grayson Warren Brown (b. 1948), *A Mass for a Soulful People*

Heav - en and earth are filled with your glo - ry.
Ho - san - na in the high - est.
Bless - ed is He who comes in the name

of the Lord, of the Lord.
Ho - san - na in the high - est, ho - san - na in the high - est.

Holy, Holy, Holy

Leader
(piano)
Ho - ly,
Ho - ly, ho - ly, ho - ly Lord, God of
pow'r _ and might, heav - en and earth are full of your glo - ry.
Ho - san - na in the high - est. Bless - ed is he who
comes in the name of the Lord. Ho - san - na in the high - est. ___

Music: Betty Carr Pulkingham (b. 1928), *Freedom Mass*. Based on traditional African melodies.

MEMORIAL ACCLAMATION

Therefore We Proclaim the Mystery of Faith

257

There-fore we pro - claim the mys - ter - y of faith;
Christ has died. Christ is
ri - sen. Christ will come a - gain al - le - lu - ia!

Music: Clarence Jos. Rivers; Accomp. Edward Stanton Cottle; choral arr. William Foster McDaniel

 Composer intends a threefold repetition: unison, S.A.T.B., congregation and S.A.T.B.

258 Christ Has Died

Christ has died. Christ is risen. Christ will come again.

Music: Marjorie Gabriel-Burrow

259 Christ Has Died

(piano)
Leader
Christ has died.
Christ has died.
Christ is ris - en. Christ will come a - gain.

Music: Betty Carr Pulkingham (b. 1928), *Freedom Mass*. Based on traditional African melodies.

We Remember His Death

We re - mem - ber His death,
We pro - claim His re - su - rect -
- ion,
We a - wait His com - ing in
1.
glo - ry.
We re -
2.
glo - ry.

Music: Hezekiah Brinson, Jr. (b. 1958)

AMEN

Amen

261

A - men, A - men,
A - men, A - men,
A - men, A - men, A - men.

Music: Carl MaultsBy, *The Saint Mary Mass*, Copyright © 1989 Malted Milk Music. Used by Permission.

Amen

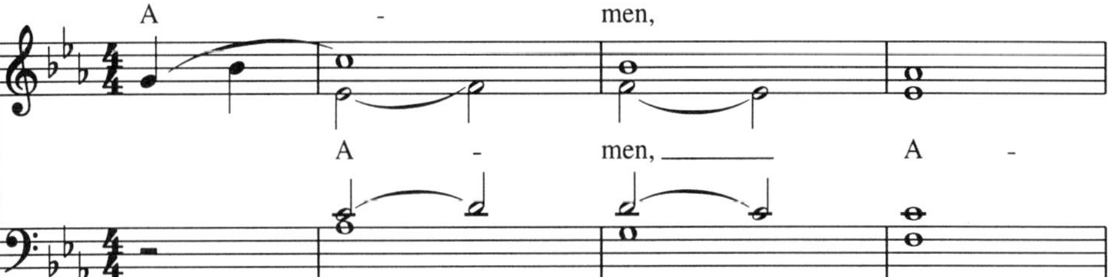
A - men,
A - men, A -

men, A - men.

Music: Roland M. Carter (b. 1942)

THE LORD'S PRAYER

263

The Lord's Prayer

Our Fa - ther in heav - en, hal - lowed be your
Name, your king-dom come, your will be done, on
earth as in heav - en. Give us to - day our
dai - ly bread. For - give us our sins as we for-give

Music: Lena McLin, *Eucharist of the Soul*
Reprinted from *Eucharist of the Soul* (GC41)

those who sin a - gainst us.
Save us
from the time of trial, and de - li - ver us from e - vil.
For the king - dom, the pow - er, and the glo - ry are
yours, now and for - ev - er. A - men.

The Lord's Prayer

Unison
Our Fa - ther, which art in heav - en, hal - low - ed
be thy name, Thy king - dom come,
Thy will be done on earth as it is in
heav - en. Give us this day our dai - ly

Music: Albert Hay Malotte; arr. Fred. Bock

bread. And for - give us our debts as we for-give our
debt-ors. And lead us not in-to temp-ta - tion, but de - liv-er us from
e - vil. For thine is the king - dom, and the pow - er, and the
glo - ry, for - ev - er. A - men.

The Lord's Prayer

Unison
Our Father in heaven, hallowed be your Name, your
kingdom come, your will be done, on earth as in heaven.
Harmony
Give us today our daily bread. Forgive us our sins as we for-

Music: Carl Haywood (b. 1949), from *Mass for Grace*, Copyright © 1992.

give those who sin a-gainst us. Save us from the time of tri - al, and de -
liv - er us from e - vil.
unison
For the king-dom, the pow - er, and the
unison
glo - ry are yours, now and for - ev - er. A - men.

The Lord's Praye

Leader
Our Fa - ther in hea - ven, hal - lowed be, hal - lowed be your Name, your king - dom come, your will be
our dai - ly bread. For - give us our sins as we for - give, for - give
from the time of trial, and de - liv - er us from e - vil. For the king - dom, the
Our Fa - ther in hea - ven, hal - lowed be, hal - lowed be your Name, your king - dom come, your will be
Give us to - day our dai - ly bread. For - give us our sins as we for - give, for - give
Save us from the time of trial, and de - liv - er us from e - vil. For the king - dom, the
Last time

Music: Betty Carr Pulkingham (b. 1928), *Freedom Mass*. Based on traditional African Melodies.

done, on earth as in heav - en. Give us to-day
those who sin a - gainst us. Save us
done, on earth as in heav - en.
those, those who sin a - gainst us.
power, and the glo - ry are yours, now and for - ev -
power, and the glo - ry are yours,
- er, A - men.
now and for - ev - er. A - men.

The Lord's Prayer

Our Father, who are in heaven,
hallowed be thy Name, Thy kingdom come, Thy will be
done, on earth as it is in heaven.
Give us this day our daily bread. Forgive us our trespass-

Music: Garfield Rochard

es, As we for-give those who tres - pass a-gainst us,
as we for - give, And lead us not in - to temp -
ta - tion, but de - li - ver us from e - vil. And lead us
not in-to temp-ta - tion, but de - li - ver us from e - vil.

FRACTION ANTHEMS

268

Christ Our Passover

Fine
Al-le-lu-ia, Al-le-lu-ia, Al-le-lu-ia.
Fine
Leader
Christ our pass-o-ver is sac-ri-ficed _ for us;
Response
(organ)
There-fore let _ us _ keep the

Music: Lena McLin, *Eucharist of the Soul*
Reprinted from *Eucharist of the Soul* (GC41)

Leader
Christ our pass - o - ver is sac - ri - ficed _ for us;
feast.
(organ)
Leader
Christ our pass-o-ver is sac-ri -
Response
There - fore let _ us _ keep the feast.
(organ)
D.C.
ficed _ for us;
Response
D.C.
There - fore let _ us _ keep the feast

Lamb of Go

Lamb of ___ God, you
take a - way the sins of the world: have mer-cy on us.
Lamb of ___ God, you take a - way the

Music: Lena McLin, *Eucharist of the Soul*
Reprinted from *Eucharist of the Soul* (GC41)

sins of the world: have mer-cy on us.
Lamb of God, you take a-way the
sins of the world: grant us peace.

Lamb of
God, you take a - way the sins of the
world: have mer - cy on us.
Lamb of
God, you take a - way the sins of the

Music: Marjorie Landsmark-DeLewis (b. 1930)

world: have mer - cy on us. Lamb of
God, you take a - way the sins of the
world: grant us peace.

Lamb of God

Leader
Respons
Lamb of God, you take a - way the sins of the world: have

Leader
Respons
mer-cy on us, Lamb of God, you take a-way the sins of the world: have

Music: Eugene W. Hancock (b. 1929)

Leader
mer - cy on us. Lamb of God, you take a-way the sins of the world:
Response
grant us peace.

1. Do this in re-mem-brance of me.
2. Eat this in re-mem-brance of me.
3. Drink this in re-mem-brance of me.
1. Do this in re - mem - brance of me.
2. Eat this in re - mem - brance of me.
3. Drink this in re - mem - brance of me.
I hung out on a tree

Music: Glenn Burleigh

for thee, for thee,
1.,2.
3.
1. Do this in re - mem - brance of me.
2. Eat this in re - mem - brance of me.
3. Drink this in re - mem - brance of me.

273

Refrain: **His Love Is Everlasting**

Suggested Use: Easter, General

His love, His love, His
love is ev - er - last - ing.

Psalm 126

1. When the Lord restored the fortunes of **Zi**on,*
   then were we like those who **dream**.
2. Then was our mouth filled with **laugh**ter,*
   and our tongue with shouts of **joy**. *Refrain*
3. Then they said among the **na**tions,*
   "The Lord has done great things for **them**."
4. The Lord has done great things for **us**,*
   and we are glad in**deed.**

† 5. Restore our fortunes, O **Lord**,*
   like the watercourses of the **Ne**gev. *Refrain*

6. Those who sowed with **tears***
   will reap with songs of **joy**.
7. Those who go out weeping, carrying the **seed**,*
   will come again with joy, shouldering their **sheaves**. *Refrain*

† (repeat second half of chant)

Refrain: Leon C. Roberts (1950-1999). Refrain: © 1987 Leon Roberts.
Simplified Anglican Chant: Carl Haywood (b. 1949), from *Mass for Grace*; Chant: © 1992 Carl Haywood.

Refrain: I Will Praise Your Name

Suggested Use: Easter, General

I will praise your name for ever, my King and my God.

Psalm 145: 8-13

8. The Lord is gracious and full of com**pas**sion,*
   slow to anger and of great **kind**ness.
9. The Lord is loving to **every**one*
   and his compassion is over all his **works**. *Refrain*
10. All your works praise you, O **Lord**,*
    and your faithful servants **bless** you.
11. They make known the glory of your **king**dom*
    and speak of your **pow**er; *Refrain*
12. That the peoples may know of your **pow**er*
    and the glorious splendor of your **king**dom.
13. Your kingdom is an everlasting **king**dom;*
    your dominion endures throughout all **a**ges. *Refrain*

Refrain: Leon C. Roberts (1950-1999).
Simplified Anglican Chant: Robert Knox Kennedy.

Refrain: **Lord, Send Out Your Spirit**

Suggested Use: Pentecost, Rogation Days

Lord, send out your spir - it!
Lord, send out your spir - it!
until **Final ending**
Lord, send out your spir - it! And re - new the face of the earth.

Refrain: Rawn Harbor (b. 1947). Used by Permission.
Simplified Anglican Chant: Jerome Webster Meachen. Permission Requested.

Final ending.
earth.

Psalm 104: 25-26, 28-32, 35

25. O Lord, how manifold are your **works**!*
in wisdom you have made them all; the earth is full of your **crea**tures.

26. Yonder is the great and wide sea with its living things too many to **num**ber,*
creatures both small and **great**. *Refrain*

28. All of them look to **you***
to give them their food in due **sea**son.

29. You give it to them; they **ga**ther it;*
you open your hand, and they are filled with good **things**. *Refrain*

30. You hide your face, and they are **terri**fied;*
you take away their breath, and they die and return to their **dust**.

31. You send forth your Spirit, and they are cre**ated;***
and so you renew the face of the **earth**. *Refrain*

32. May the glory of the Lord endure for**ever**;*
may the Lord rejoice in all his **works**.

35. May these words of mine **please** him;*
I will rejoice in the **Lord**. *Refrain*

Refrain: **My God, Why Have You Abandoned Me?**

Suggested Use: Palm Sunday, Good Friday

My God, my God, why have you a - ban - doned me?

Refrain: Rawn Harbor (b. 1947). Used by Permission.
Simplified Anglican Chant: Carl Haywood (b. 1949), from *Mass for Grace*, Copyright © 1992.

Psalm 22: 1-2, 7-8, 14-21

1. My God, My God, why have youe for**sak**en me?*
 and are so far from my cry and from the words of my dis**tress**?
2. O my God, I cry in the daytime, but you do not **an**swer;*
 by night as well, but I find no **rest**.
7. All who see me laugh me to **scorn**;*
 they curl their lips and wag their heads, **say**ing,
8. "He trusted in the Lord; let him de**liv**er him;*
 let him rescue him, if he de**lights** in him." *Refrain*
14. I am poured out like water; all my bones are out of **joint**;*
 my heart within my breast is melting **wax**.
15. My mouth is dried out like a pot-sherd;
 my tongue sticks to the roof of my **mouth**;*
 and you have laid me in the dust of the **grave**. *Refrain*
16. Packs of dogs close me in, and gangs of evildoers circle a**round** me;*
 they pierce my hands and my feet; I can count my **bones**.
17. They stare and gloat **over** me;*
 they divide my garments among them; they cast lots for my **cloth**ing.
18. Be not far away, O **Lord**;*
 you are my strength; hasten to **help** me.
19. Save me from the **sword**,*
 my life from the power of the **dog**. *Refrain*
20. Save me from the lion's **mouth,***
 my wretched body from the horns of wild **bulls**.
21. I will declare your Name to my **breth**ren;
 in the midst of the congregation I will **praise** you. *Refrain*

Refrain: The Lord Is My Light and My Salvation

Suggested Use: Epiphany, General

The Lord is my light and my sal - va - tion.

Refrain: Leon C. Roberts (1950-1999). Refrain: © 1987 Leon Roberts.
Anglican Chant: Clarence Witeman. Chant © Clarence Earl Whiteman.

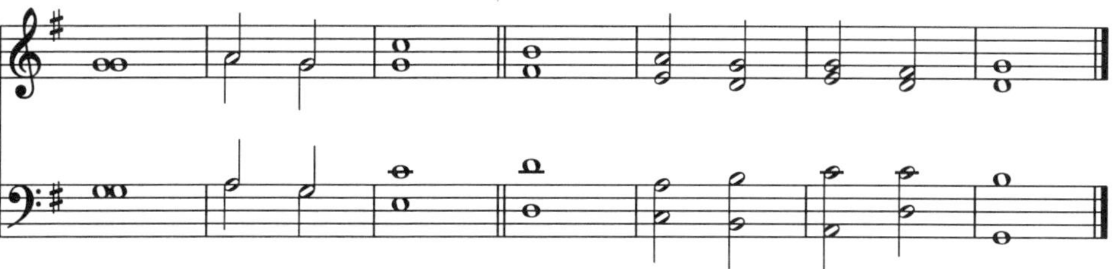

Psalm 27: 1-9

1. The Lord is my light and my salvation; whom then ' shall I ' fear?*
   the Lord is the strength of my life; of whom then ' shall I ' be a ' fraid?

2. When evildoers came upon me to eat ' up my ' flesh,*
   it was they, my foes and my ' adversaries, who ' stumbled and ' fell. *Refrain*

3. Though an army should en ' camp a ' gainst me,*
   yet my ' heart shall not ' be a ' fraid;

4. And though war should rise ' up a ' gainst me,*
   yet will I ' put my ' trust in ' Him. *Refrain*

5. One thing have I asked of the Lord; ' one thing I ' seek;*
   that I may dwell in the house of the ' Lord all the ' days of my ' life;

6. To behold the fair ' beauty of the ' Lord*
   and to ' seek him ' in his ' temple. *Refrain*

7. For in the day of trouble he shall keep me ' safe in his ' shelter;*
   he shall hide me in the secrecy of his dwelling
   and set me ' high up ' on a ' rock.

8. Even now he lifts ' up my ' head*
   above my ' enemies ' round a ' bout me.

9. Therefore I will offer in his dwelling an oblation
   with ' sounds of great ' gladness;*
   I will sing and make ' music ' to the ' Lord. *Refrain*

Suggested Use: Easter, General

Serve the Lord with glad - ness, al - le - lu - ia.

(organ)

Psalm 100: 1-4

1. O be joyful in the | Lord all ye | lands;*
   serve the Lord with gladness
   and come before his | presence | with a | song. *Refrain*

2. Be ye sure that the Lord he is God;
   it is he that hath made us and not | we our | selves;*
   we are his | people and the | sheep of his | pasture. *Refrain*

3. O go your way into his gates with thanksgiving
   and into his | courts with | praise;*
   be thankful unto | him and speak | good of his | Name. *Refrain*

4. For the Lord is gracious;
   his mercy is | ever | lasting;*
   and his truth endureth from gener | ation to | gener | ation. *Refra*

Soprano descant (after Verse 4)

Al - le - lu - ia, al - le - lu - ia.

Refrain: The Lord Is My Shepherd

Suggested Use: Lent, Easter, Baptism, Burial

The Lord is my shep - herd;
there is noth - ing I shall want.

Psalm 23

1. The Lord is my **shep**herd;*
   I shall not **want**.
2. He maketh me to lie down in green **pas**tures;*
   he leadeth me beside the still **wa**ters. *Refrain*
3. He restoreth my **soul**;*
   he leadeth me in the paths of righteousness for His Name's **sake**.
4. Yea, though I walk through the valley of the shadow of death,
   I will fear no **evil**;*
   for thou are with me; thy rod and thy staff they **com**fort me. *Refrain*
5. Thou preparest a table before me in the presence of mine **en**emies;*
   thou anointest my head with oil; my cup runneth **over**.
6. Surely goodness and mercy shall follow me all the days of my **life**,*
   and I will dwell in the house of the Lord for**ever**. *Refrain*

efrain: Leon C. Roberts (1950-1999). Refrain: © 1987 Leon Roberts.
mplified Anglican Chant: Robert Knox Kennedy. Chant used by permission.

Refrain: **To You, O Lord**

Suggested Use: Advent, Ascension

To you, O Lord, I lift up my
soul, to on-ly you, O Lord;
I wait for your re - turn.

Refrain: Rawn Harbor (b. 1947). Used by Permission.
Simplified Anglican Chant: Curtis Sisco (1958-1992)

Psalm 24: 1-10

1. The earth is the Lord's and all that is **in** it,*
   the world and all who dwell there**in**.
2. For it is he who founded it upon the **seas***
   and made it firm upon the rivers of the **deep**. *Refrain*
3. "Who can ascend the hill of the **Lord**?*
   and who can stand in his holy **place**?"
4. "Those who have clean hands and a pure **heart**,*
   who have not pledged themselves to falsehood,
   nor sworn by what is a **fraud**. *Refrain*
5. They shall receive a blessing from the **Lord***
   and a just reward from the God of their sal**va**tion."
6. Such is the generation of those who seek **him**,*
   of those who seek your face, O God of **Jac**ob. *Refrain*
7. Lift up your heads, O gates; lift them high, O everlasting **doors**;*
   and the King of glory shall come **in**.
8. "Who is this King of **glo**ry?"*
   "The Lord, strong and mighty, the Lord, mighty in **bat**tle." *Refrain*
9. Lift up your heads, O gates; lift them high, O everlasting **doors;***
   and the King of glory shall come **in**.
10. "Who is He, this King of **glo**ry?"*
    "The Lord of hosts, he is the King of **glo**ry." *Refrain*

English 1. Bless, O Lord, our coun - try, Af - ri - ca. So that she may wak - en
Swahili 2. Bwa - na, i - ba - ri - ki Af - ri - ka, I - li - i - pa - te
Zulu 3. Nko - si si - kel - el' i Af - ri - ka, Mal - u - pa-kam' u - pon -
from her sleep. Fill her horn with plen - ty, guide her feet.
ku - am - ka. Ma - om - bi ye ta ya - si - ki - lel.
do - lway - o; Yi - va im - i - tan - da - zo ye - tu.
Fine
Hear us, faith - ful ones Spir - it, de - scend, (Spir - it, Spir - it.)
U - tu - ba - ri - ki. U - je Ro - ho, (U - je, U - je.)
U - si - si - kel - el - e, Yih la Moy - a, (Yih - la Mo - ya.)
Spir - it, de-scend, Spir - it, de- scend, Spir - it di - vine.
U - je Ro - ho. U - je Ro - ho. U - tu - ja - ze.
Yih - la Moy - a. Oy - ing cwel - e.

Words: Zula-Enoch Sontonga; English, Katherine F. Rohrbough
Music: Enoch Sontonga

Indices

Indices

Composers, Harmonizers, Arrangers, and Sources for Hymns

Authors, Translators, and Sources for Hymns

Composers, Arrangers, and Sources for Service Music

Titles & First Lines